GUITAR TAB EDITION

Play Guitar With...

RORY GALLA...

IRISH TOUR

CW00742412

Wise Publications
part of The Music Sales Group

London / New York / Paris / Sydney / Copenhagen / Berlin / Madrid / Hong Kong / Tokyo

Published by
Wise Publications
14-15 Berners Street, London, W1T 3LJ, UK.

Exclusive distributors:
Music Sales Limited
Distribution Centre, Newmarket Road,
Bury St Edmunds, Suffolk, IP33 3YB, UK.

Music Sales Pty Limited
20 Resolution Drive, Caringbah, NSW 2229, Australia.

Order No. AM1009184
ISBN 978-1-78305-626-2

Edited by Adrian Hopkins.
Music arranged by Arthur Dick.
Music engraved by Paul Ewers Music Design.
All Rory Gallagher images courtesy of Strange Music Limited.
Cover design by Mark Jessett.

All audio mixed and mastered by
Jonas Persson and Imogen Hall.
All audio courtesy of Strange Music Limited.
All audio recorded at Cork City Hall, 5 January 1974.

Printed in the EU.

www.musicsales.com

Special thanks to Daniel Gallagher
for his assistance in preparing this volume.

A selection of over fifty Rory Gallagher
songs are also available to download from
www.sheetmusicdirect.com

Cradle Rock
(Gallagher)
Strange Music Limited.

Hands Off
(Gallagher)
Strange Music Limited.

I Wonder Who
(Morganfield)
Arc Music Corp/Strange Music Limited.

Messin' With The Kid
(London)
Kassner Associated Publishers Limited.

A Million Miles Away
(Gallagher)
Strange Music Limited.

Too Much Alcohol
(Hutto)
Universal Music Publishing Limited.

Who's That Coming
(Gallagher)
Strange Music Limited.

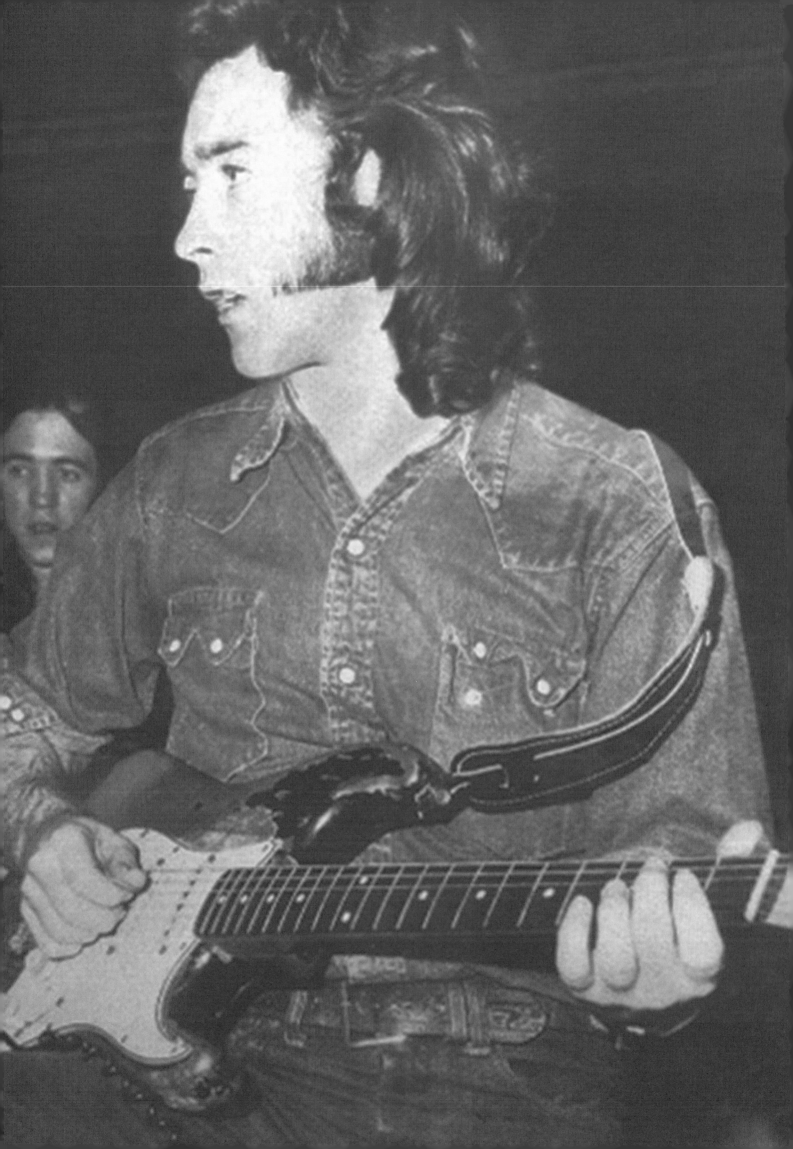

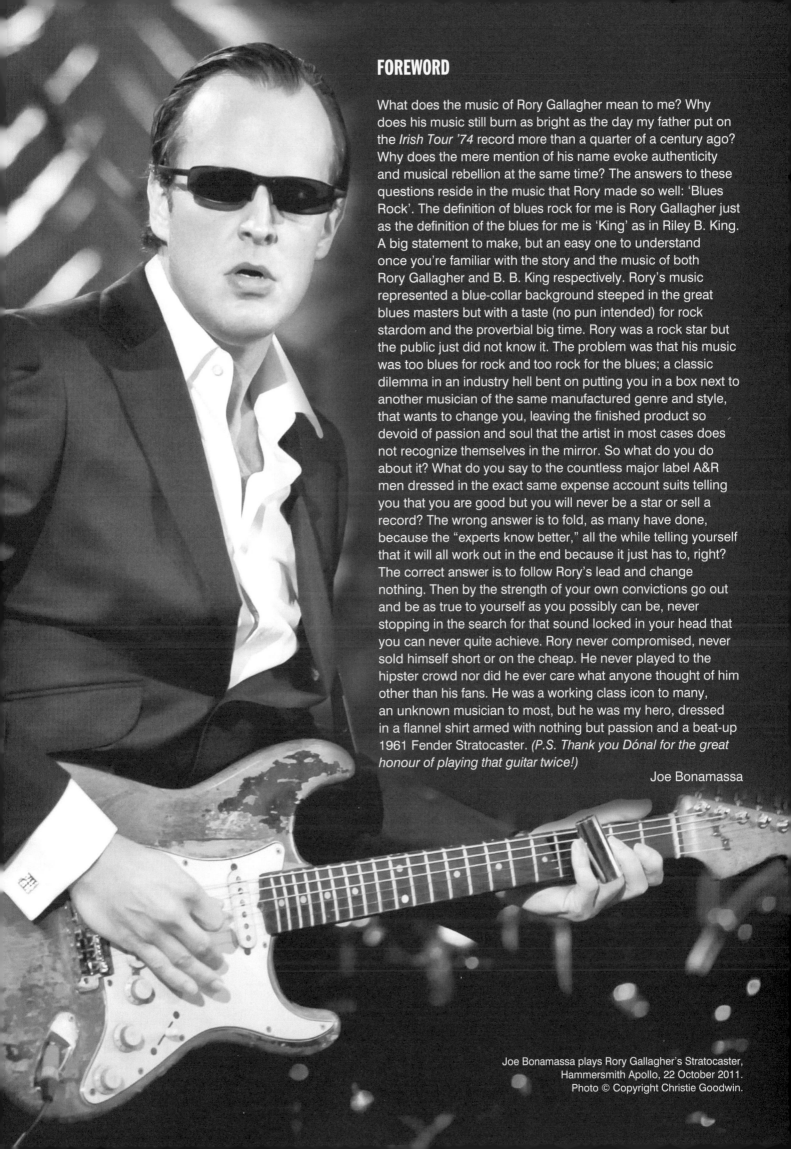

FOREWORD

What does the music of Rory Gallagher mean to me? Why does his music still burn as bright as the day my father put on the *Irish Tour '74* record more than a quarter of a century ago? Why does the mere mention of his name evoke authenticity and musical rebellion at the same time? The answers to these questions reside in the music that Rory made so well: 'Blues Rock'. The definition of blues rock for me is Rory Gallagher just as the definition of the blues for me is 'King' as in Riley B. King. A big statement to make, but an easy one to understand once you're familiar with the story and the music of both Rory Gallagher and B. B. King respectively. Rory's music represented a blue-collar background steeped in the great blues masters but with a taste (no pun intended) for rock stardom and the proverbial big time. Rory was a rock star but the public just did not know it. The problem was that his music was too blues for rock and too rock for the blues; a classic dilemma in an industry hell bent on putting you in a box next to another musician of the same manufactured genre and style, that wants to change you, leaving the finished product so devoid of passion and soul that the artist in most cases does not recognize themselves in the mirror. So what do you do about it? What do you say to the countless major label A&R men dressed in the exact same expense account suits telling you that you are good but you will never be a star or sell a record? The wrong answer is to fold, as many have done, because the "experts know better," all the while telling yourself that it will all work out in the end because it just has to, right? The correct answer is to follow Rory's lead and change nothing. Then by the strength of your own convictions go out and be as true to yourself as you possibly can be, never stopping in the search for that sound locked in your head that you can never quite achieve. Rory never compromised, never sold himself short or on the cheap. He never played to the hipster crowd nor did he ever care what anyone thought of him other than his fans. He was a working class icon to many, an unknown musician to most, but he was my hero, dressed in a flannel shirt armed with nothing but passion and a beat-up 1961 Fender Stratocaster. *(P.S. Thank you Dónal for the great honour of playing that guitar twice!)*

Joe Bonamassa

Joe Bonamassa plays Rory Gallagher's Stratocaster,
Hammersmith Apollo, 22 October 2011.
Photo © Copyright Christie Goodwin.

Guitar tablature explained

Guitar music can be explained in three different ways: on a musical stave, in tablature, and in rhythm slashes.

RHYTHM SLASHES: are written above the stave. Strum chords in the rhythm indicated. Round noteheads indicate single notes.

THE MUSICAL STAVE: shows pitches and rhythms and is divided by lines into bars. Pitches are named after the first seven letters of the alphabet.

TABLATURE: graphically represents the guitar fingerboard. Each horizontal line represents a string, and each number represents a fret.

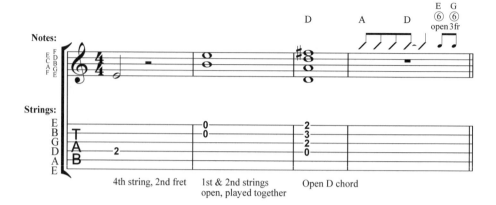

4th string, 2nd fret   1st & 2nd strings open, played together   Open D chord

Definitions for special guitar notation

SEMI-TONE BEND: Strike the note and bend up a semi-tone (½ step).

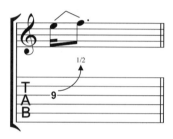

WHOLE-TONE BEND: Strike the note and bend up a whole-tone (full step).

GRACE NOTE BEND: Strike the note and bend as indicated. Play the first note as quickly as possible.

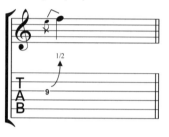

QUARTER-TONE BEND: Strike the note and bend up a ¼ step

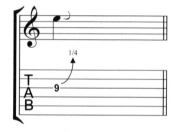

BEND & RELEASE: Strike the note and bend up as indicated, then release back to the original note.

COMPOUND BEND & RELEASE: Strike the note and bend up and down in the rhythm indicated.

PRE-BEND: Bend the note as indicated, then strike it.

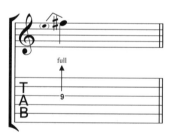

PRE-BEND & RELEASE: Bend the note as indicated. Strike it and release the note back to the original pitch.

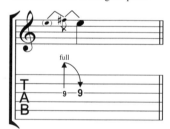

HAMMER-ON: Strike the first note with one finger, then sound the second note (on the same string) with another finger by fretting it without picking.

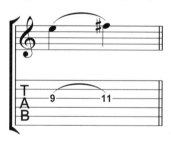

PULL-OFF: Place both fingers on the note to be sounded, strike the first note and without picking, pull the finger off to sound the second note.

LEGATO SLIDE (GLISS): Strike the first note and then slide the same fret-hand finger up or down to the second note. The second note is not struck.

MUFFLED STRINGS: A percussive sound is produced by laying the first hand across the string(s) without depressing, and striking them with the pick hand.

NATURAL HARMONIC: Strike the note while the fret-hand lightly touches the string directly over the fret indicated.

PICK SCRAPE: The edge of the pick is rubbed down (or up) the string, producing a scratchy sound.

PALM MUTING: The note is partially muted by the pick hand lightly touching the string(s) just before the bridge.

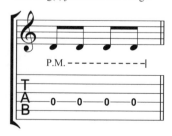

SHIFT SLIDE (GLISS & RESTRIKE) Same as legato slide, except the second note is struck.

TAP HARMONIC: The note is fretted normally and a harmonic is produced by tapping or slapping the fret indicated in brackets (which will be twelve frets higher than the fretted note.)

TAPPING: Hammer ('tap') the fret indicated with the pick-hand index or middle finger and pull-off to the note fretted by the fret hand.

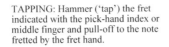

PINCH HARMONIC: The note is fretted normally and a harmonic is produced by adding the edge of the thumb or the tip of the index finger of the pick hand to the normal pick attack.

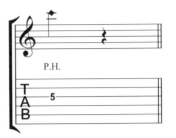

ARTIFICIAL HARMONIC: The note fretted normally and a harmonic is produced by gently resting the pick hand's index finger directly above the indicated fret (in brackets) while plucking the appropriate string.

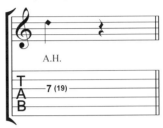

TRILL: Very rapidly alternate between the notes indicated by continuously hammering-on and pulling-off.

RAKE: Drag the pick across the strings with a single motion.

TREMOLO PICKING: The note is picked as rapidly and continously as possible.

ARPEGGIATE: Play the notes of the chord indicated by quickly rolling them from bottom to top.

SWEEP PICKING: Rhythmic downstroke and/or upstroke motion across the strings.

VIBRATO DIVE BAR AND RETURN: The pitch of the note or chord is dropped a specific number of steps (in rhythm) then returned to the original pitch.

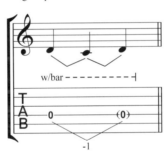

VIBRATO BAR SCOOP: Depress the bar just before striking the note, then quickly release the bar.

VIBRATO BAR DIP: Strike the note and then immediately drop a specific number of steps, then release back to the original pitch.

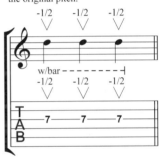

Additional musical definitions

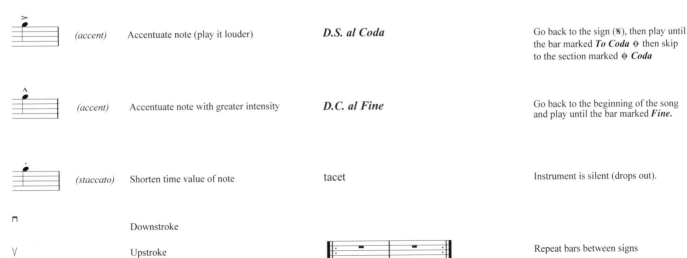

(accent)	Accentuate note (play it louder)	**D.S. al Coda**	Go back to the sign ($), then play until the bar marked **To Coda** ⊕ then skip to the section marked ⊕ **Coda**
(accent)	Accentuate note with greater intensity	**D.C. al Fine**	Go back to the beginning of the song and play until the bar marked **Fine.**
(staccato)	Shorten time value of note	tacet	Instrument is silent (drops out).
	Downstroke		
V	Upstroke		Repeat bars between signs

NOTE: Tablature numbers in brackets mean:
1. The note is sustained, but a new articulation (such as hammer-on or slide) begins
2. A note may be fretted but not necessarily played.

1. **2.** When a repeat section has different endings, play the first ending only the first time and the second ending only the second time.

MESSIN' WITH THE KID

Words & Music by Mel London

10

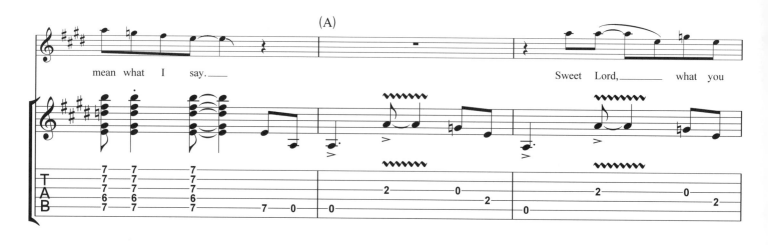

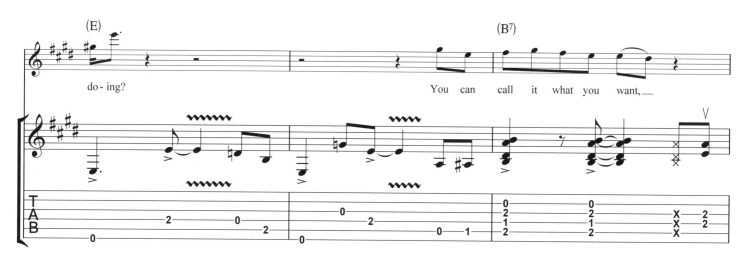

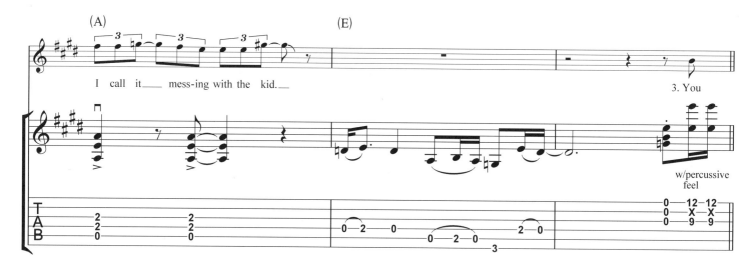

Verse

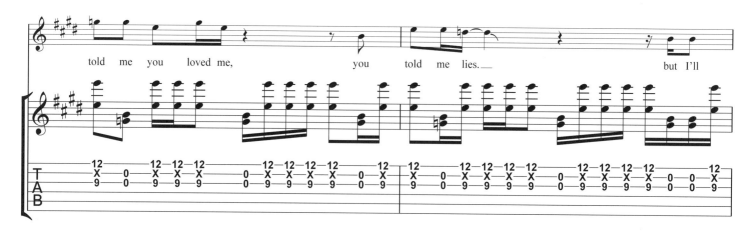

love you, darl-in' 'til the day I___ die.___

(A)

Sweet Lord,___ what you do-ing?

(E)

You can call it what you want,_

(B⁷)

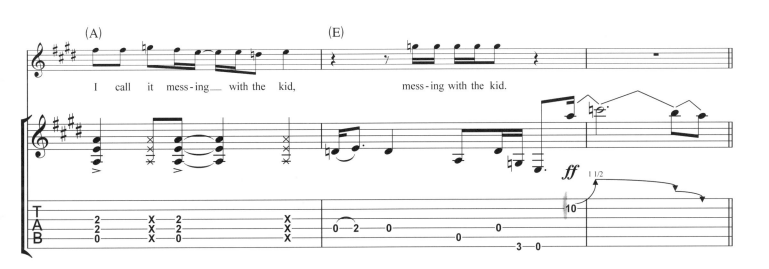

(A)

I call it mess-ing___ with the kid,

(E)

mess-ing with the kid.

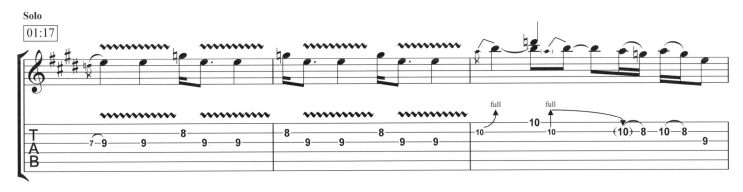

Solo

`01:17`

13

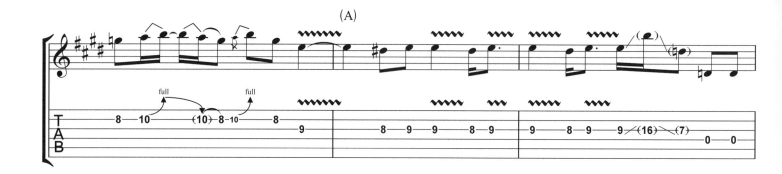

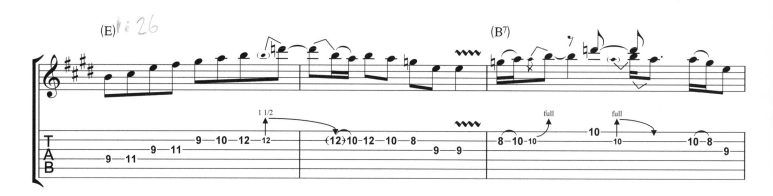

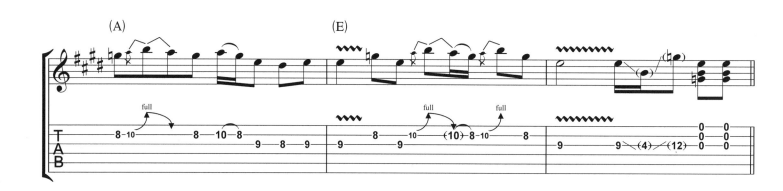

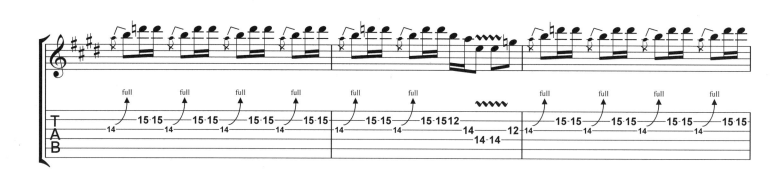

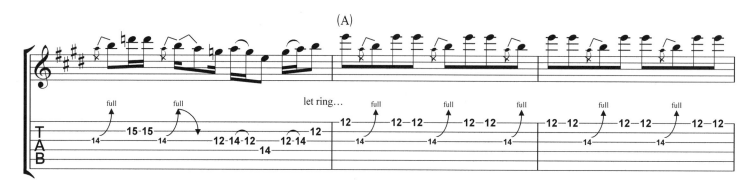

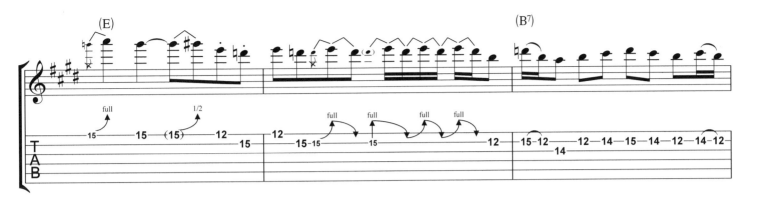

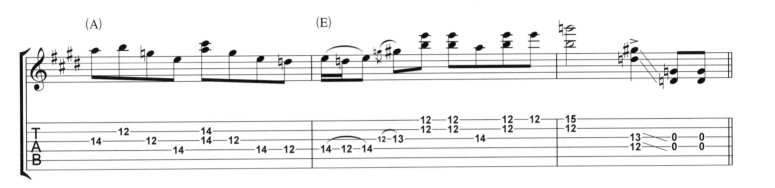

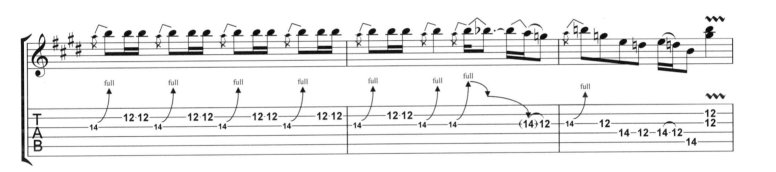

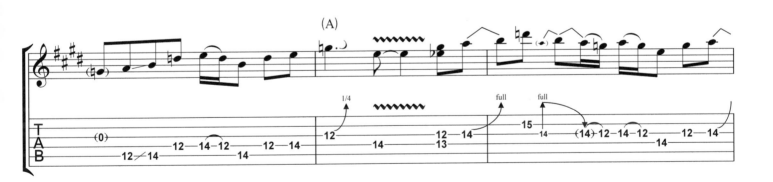

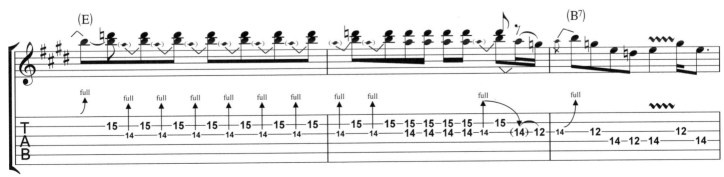

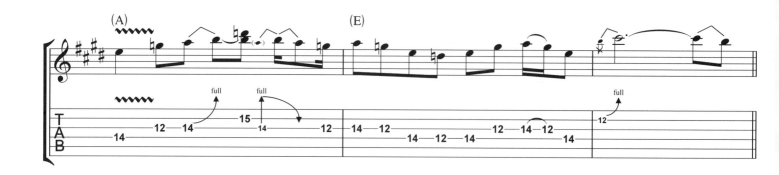

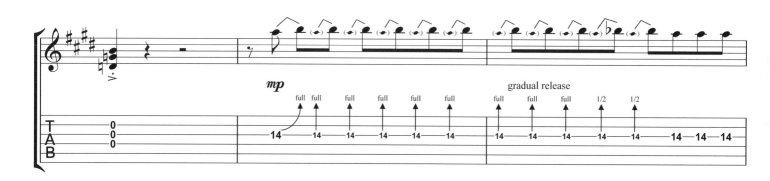

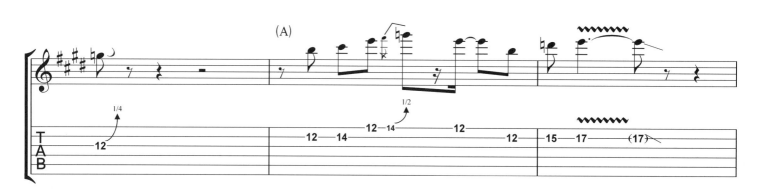

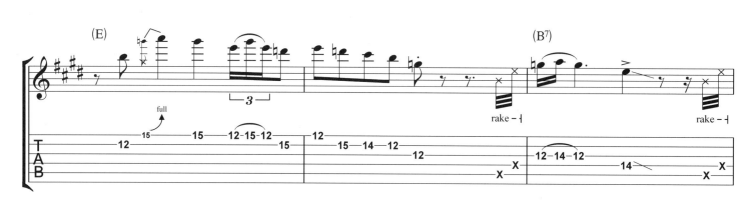

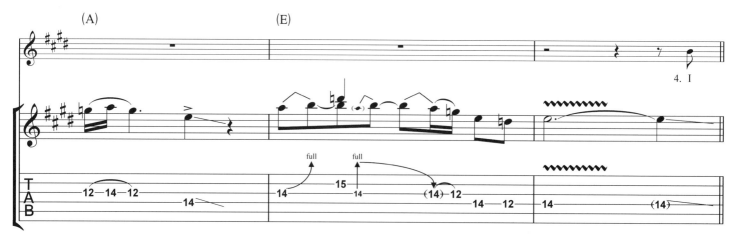

just don't talk__ but I_____ can think,__ I says what I mean, and I mean what I say,__ yeah, yeah.__

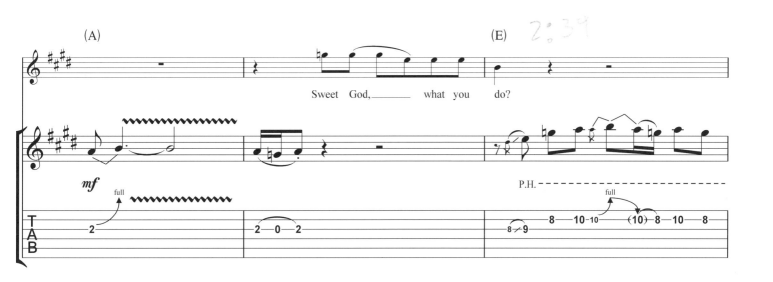

Sweet God,_____ what you do?

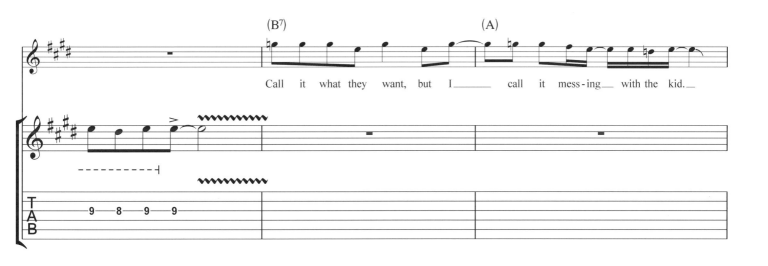

Call it what they want, but I_____ call it mess-ing__ with the kid.__

Mess- ing with the

19

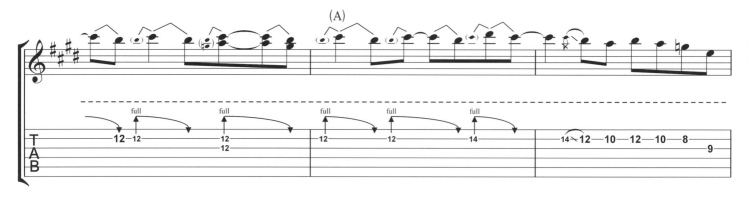

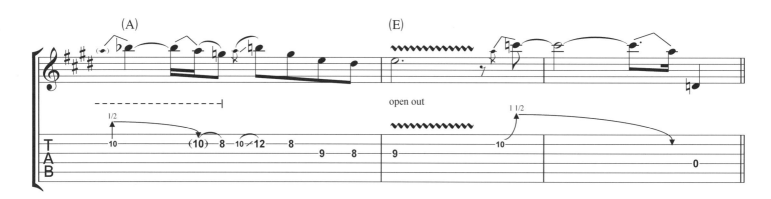

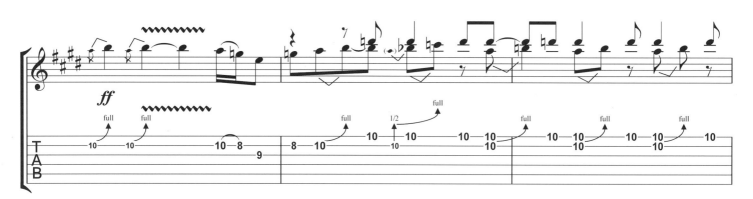

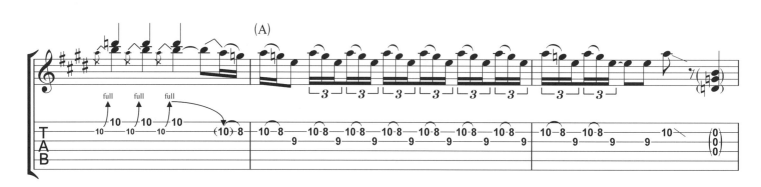

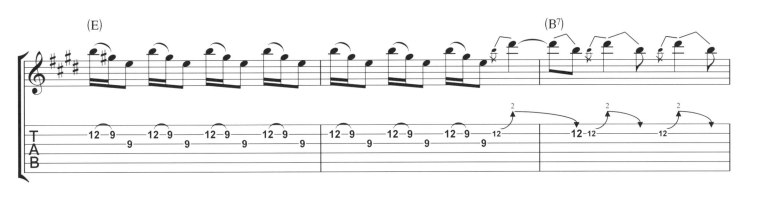

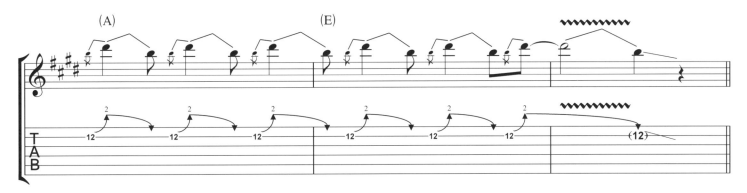

Piano Solo

03:58

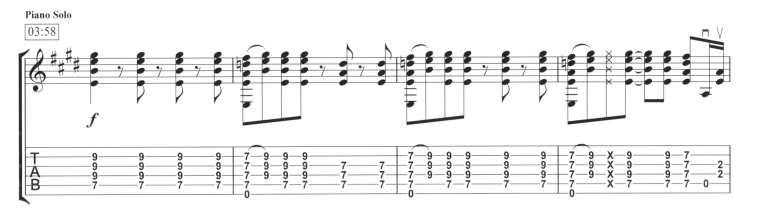

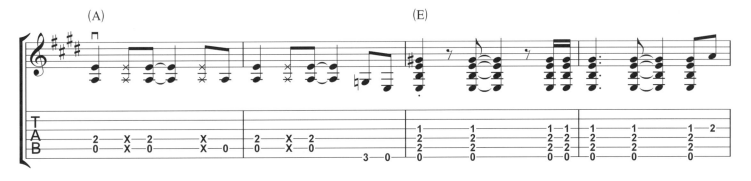

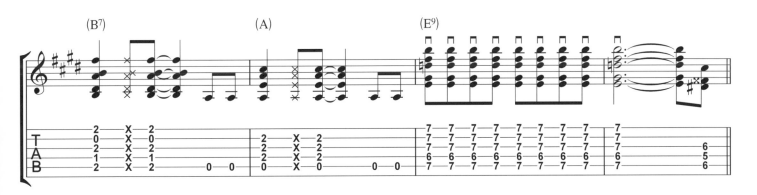

21

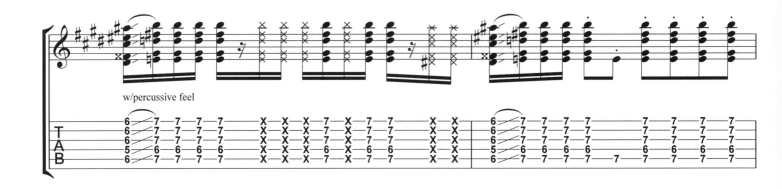

w/percussive feel

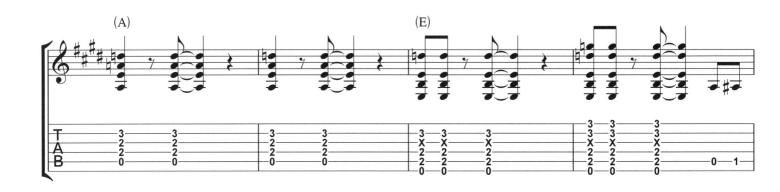

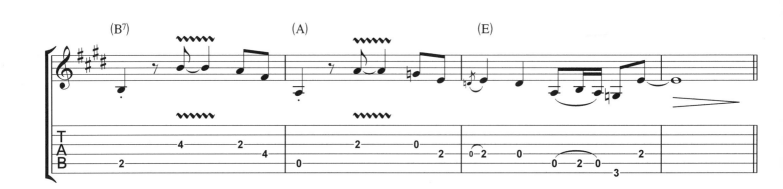

Chorus

Mess - ing with the kid,____ we've caught him mess - ing with the kid.

22

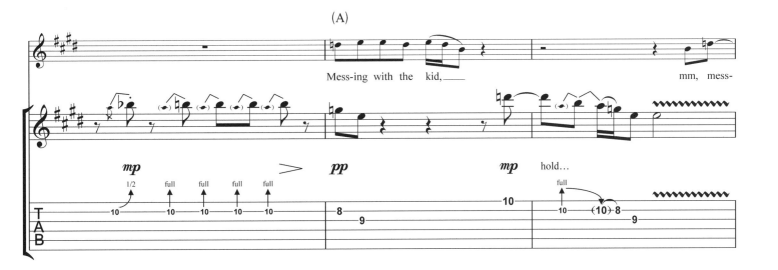

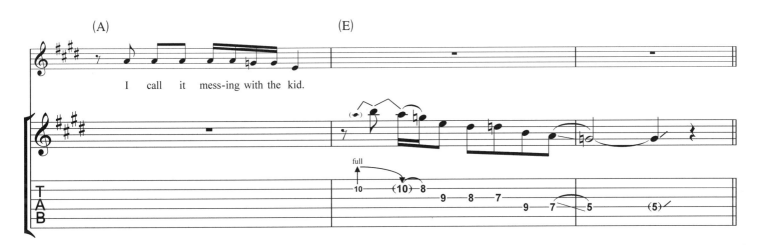

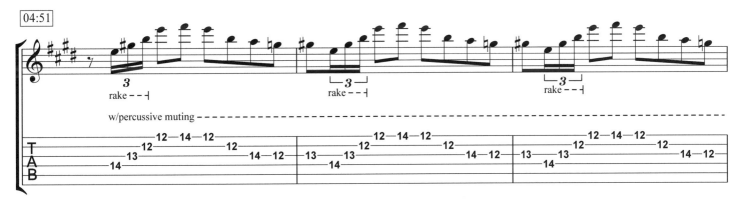

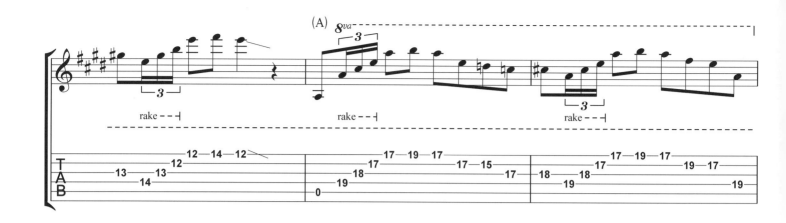

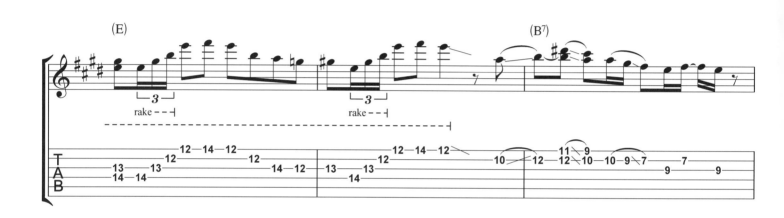

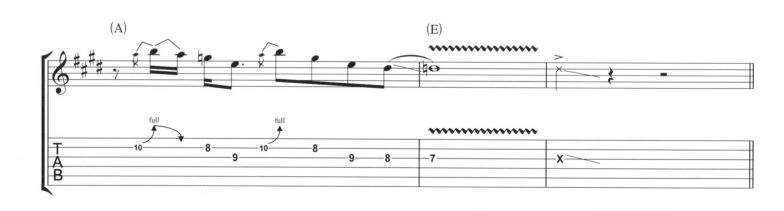

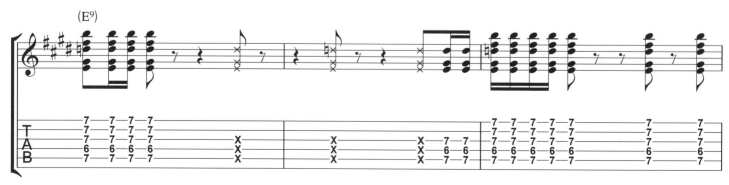

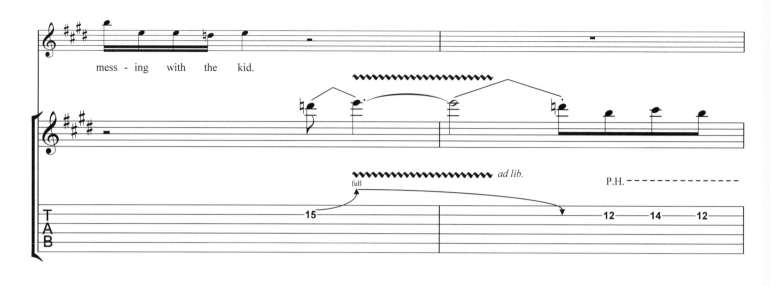

mess - ing with the kid.

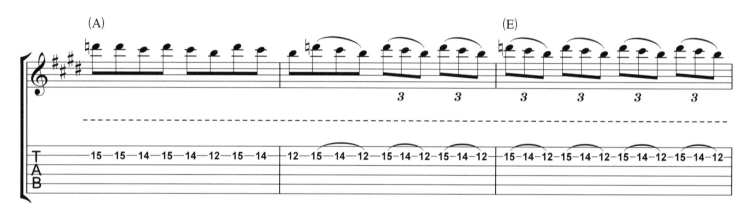

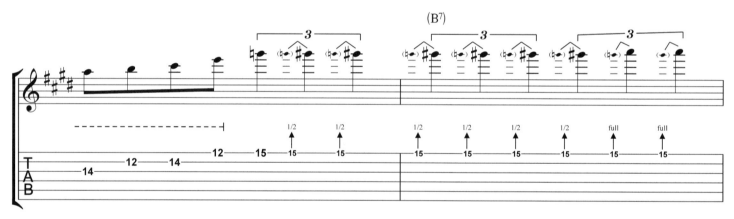

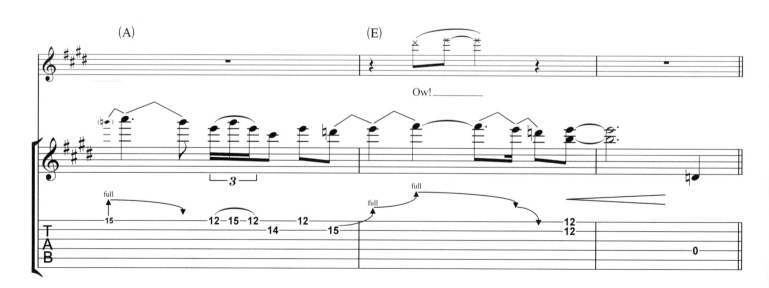

Ow!

26

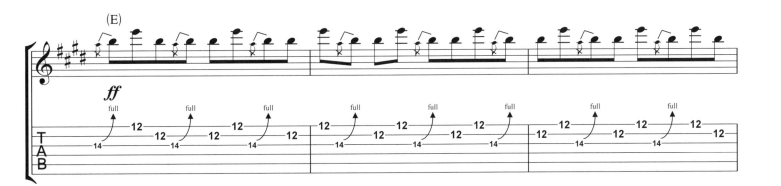

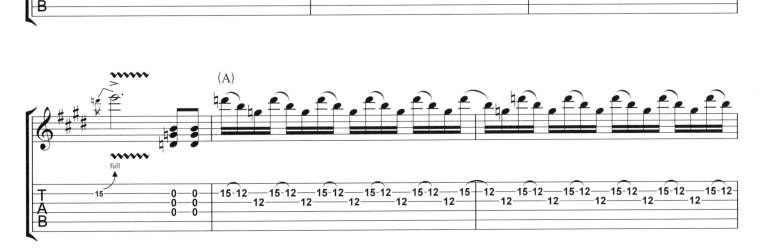

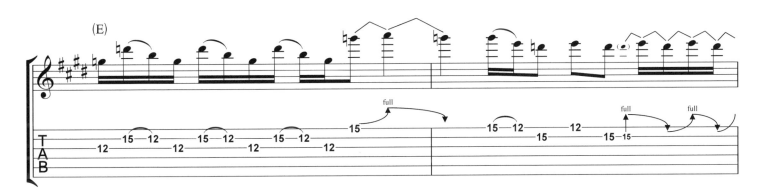

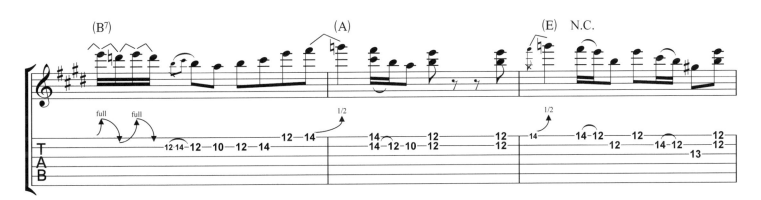

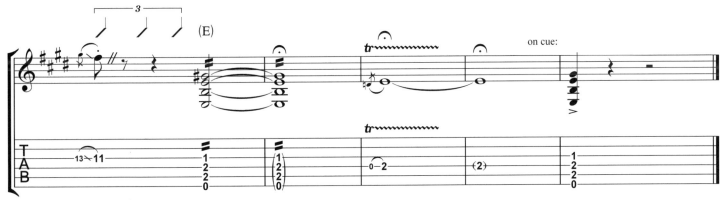

27

CRADLE ROCK

Words & Music by Rory Gallagher

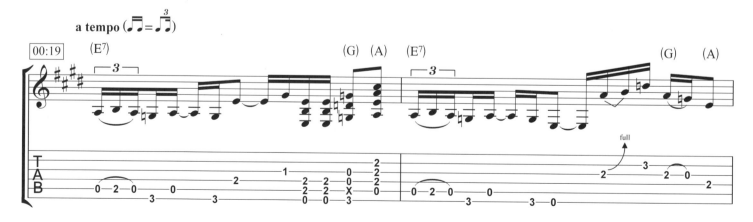

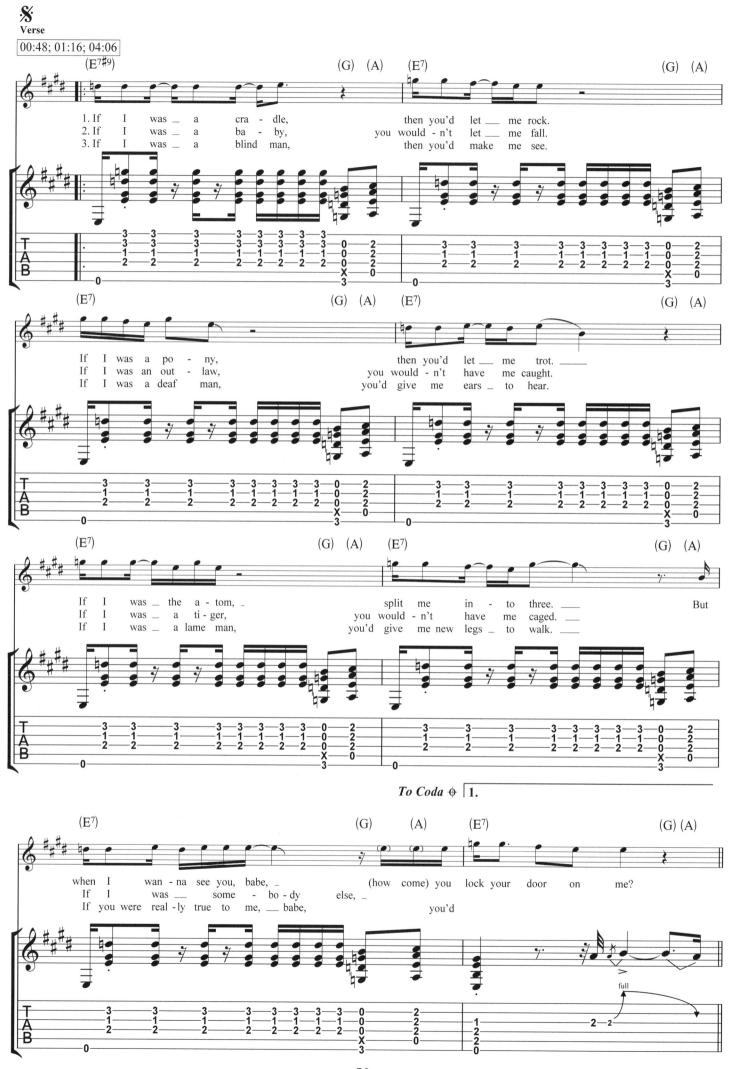

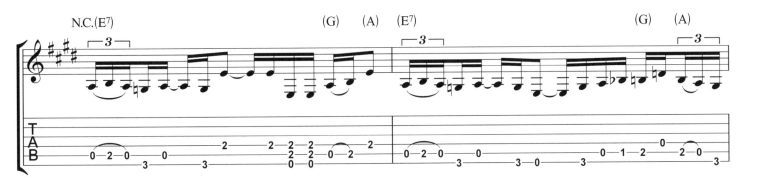

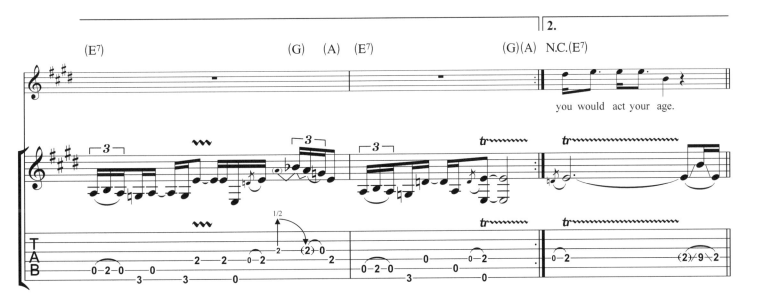

you would act your age.

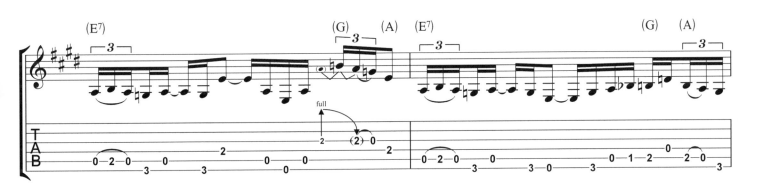

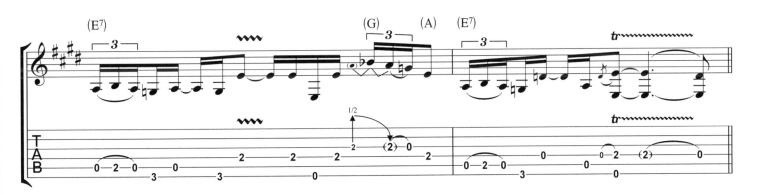

34

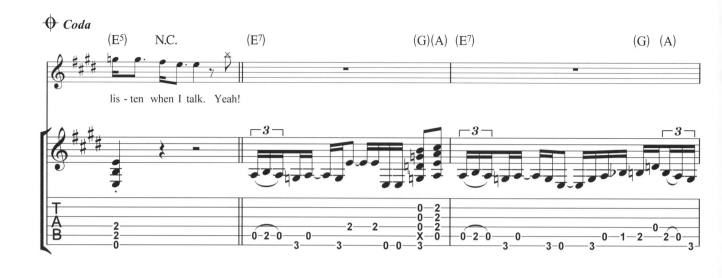

lis - ten when I talk. Yeah!

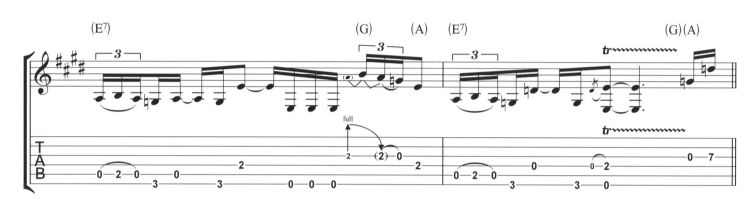

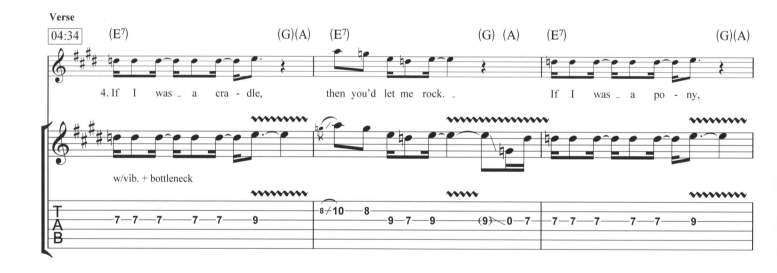

Verse

04:34

4. If I was _ a cra - dle, then you'd let me rock. _ If I was _ a po - ny,

w/vib. + bottleneck

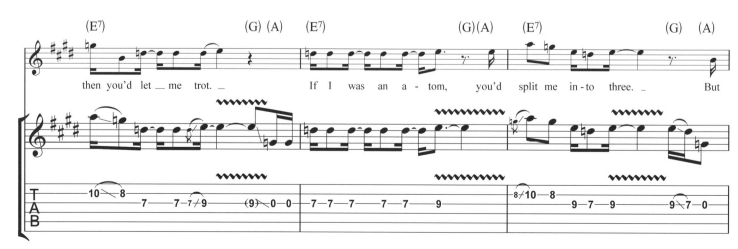

then you'd let __ me trot. _ If I was an a - tom, you'd split me in - to three. _ But

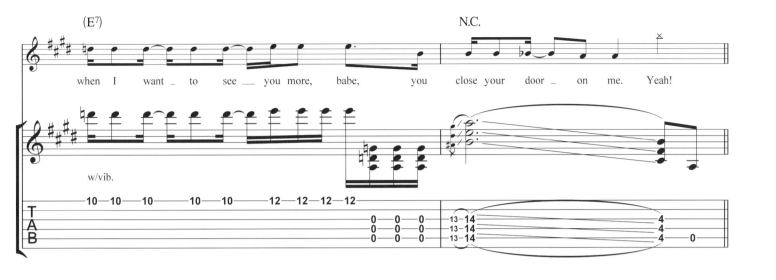

when I want to see you more, babe, you close your door on me. Yeah!

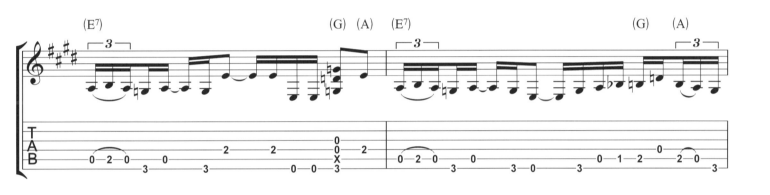

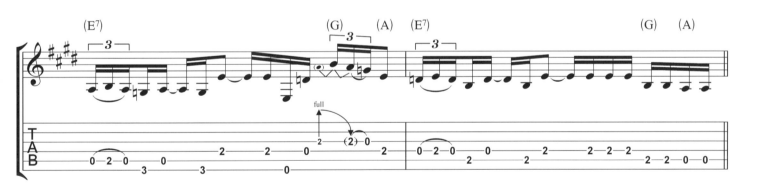

Outro solo

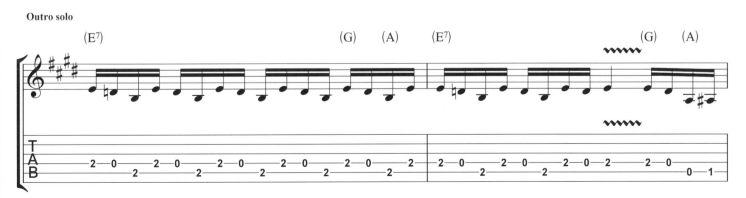

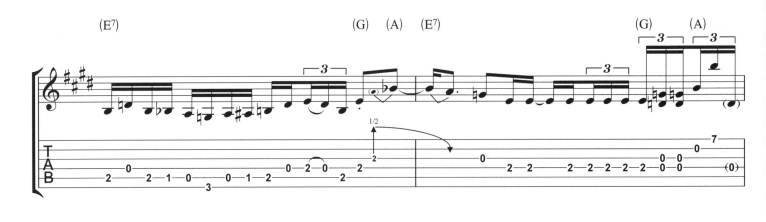

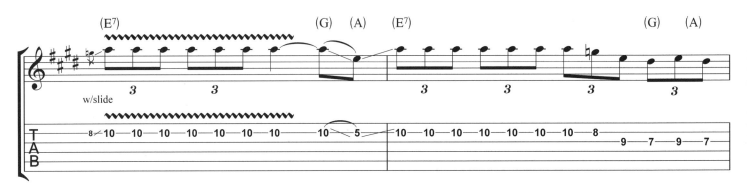

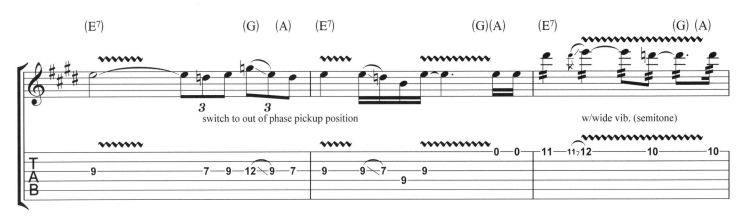

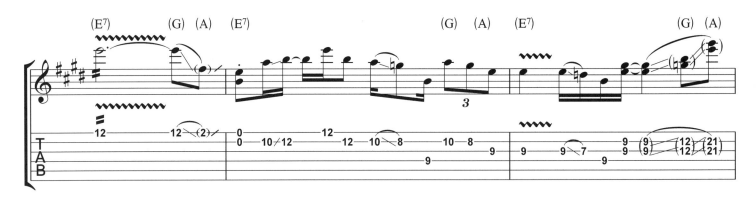

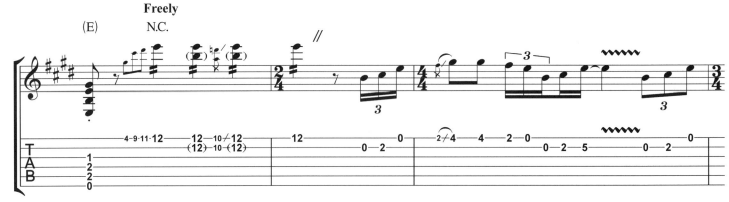

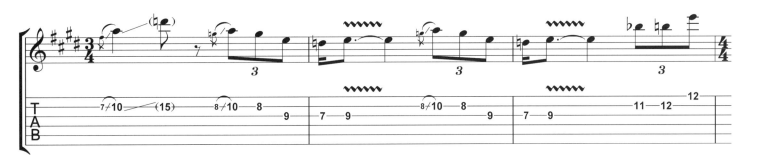

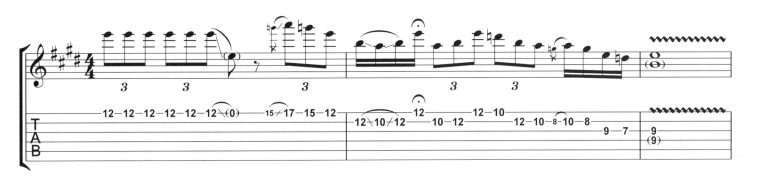

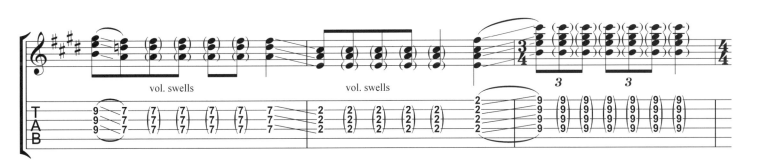

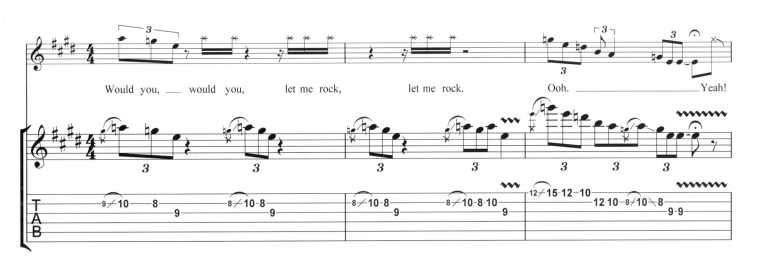

Would you, — would you, let me rock, let me rock. Ooh. _____ Yeah!

I WONDER WHO

Words & Music by McKinley Morganfield

Verse

(C⁵)

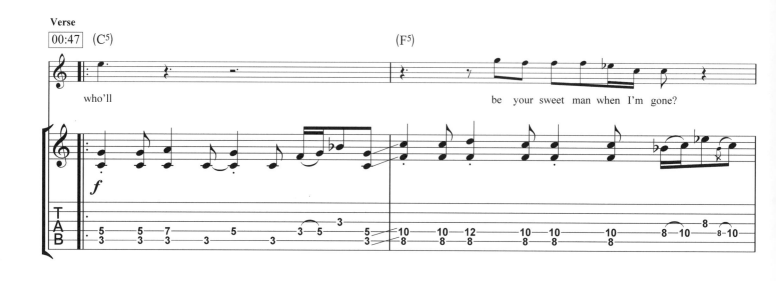

who'll be your sweet man when I'm gone?

(C⁵)

Yeah. I won-der who'll _

(F⁵)

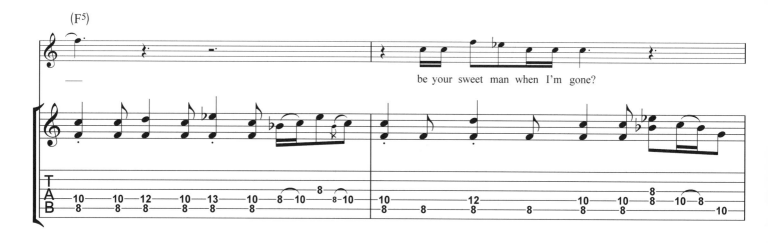

be your sweet man when I'm gone?

(C⁵)

Yeah!

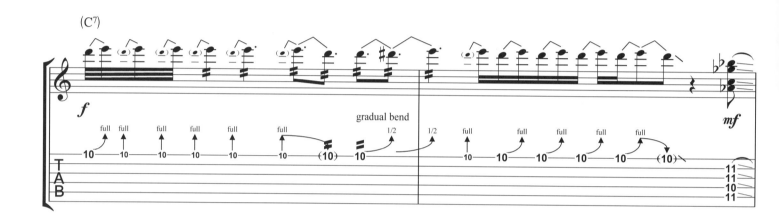

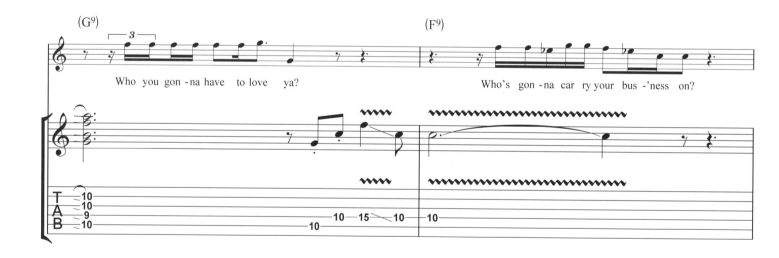

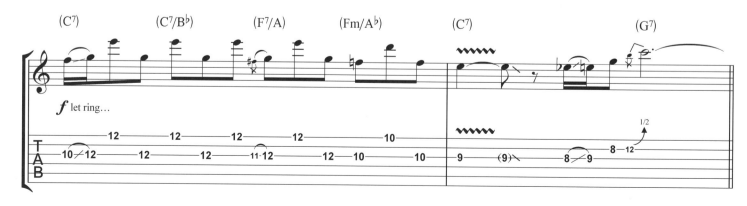

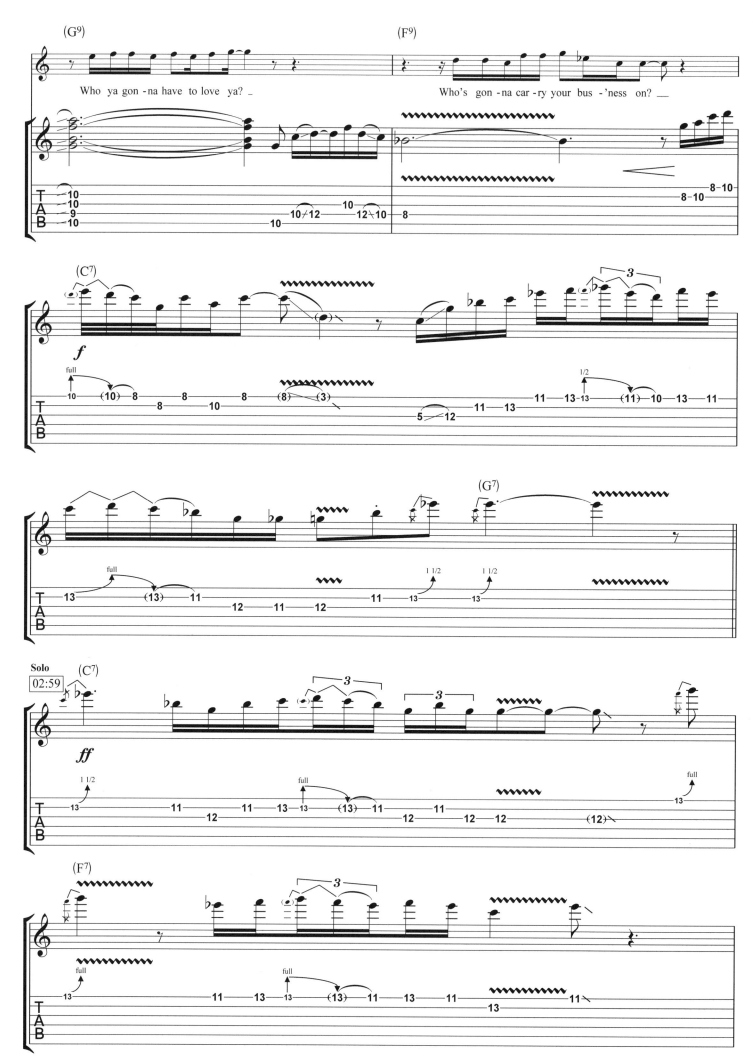

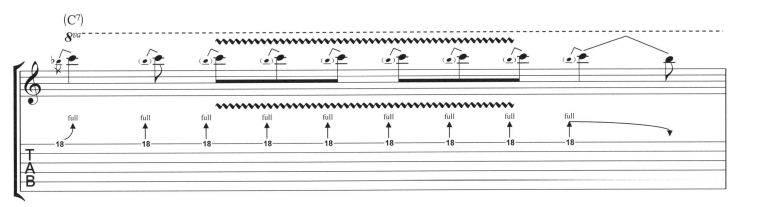

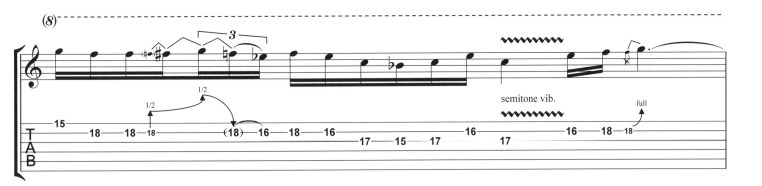

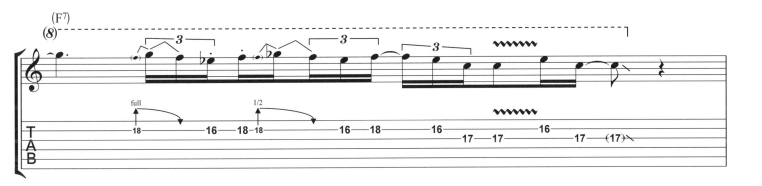

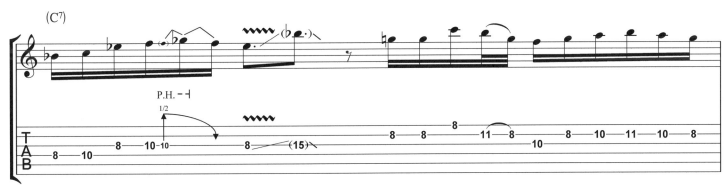

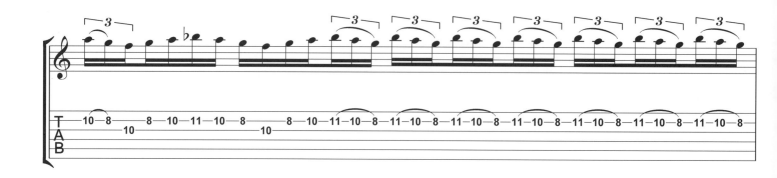

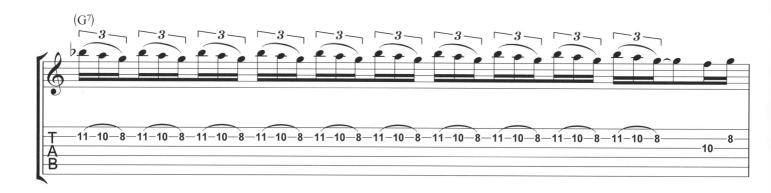

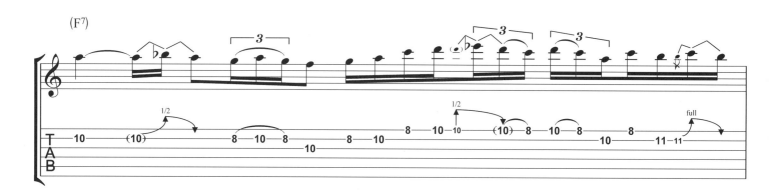

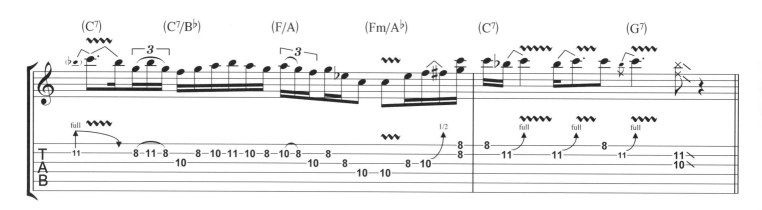

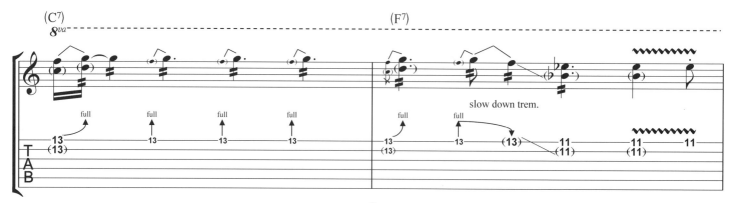

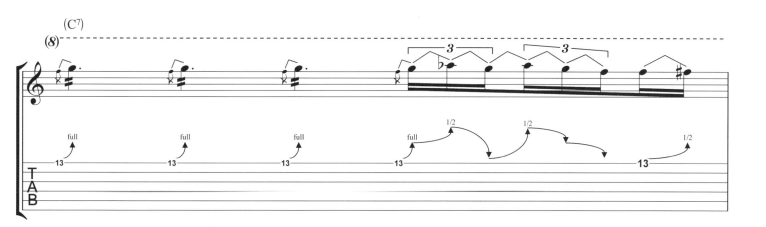

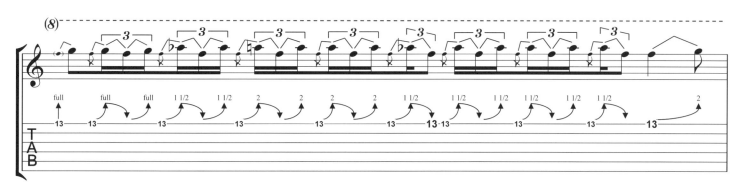

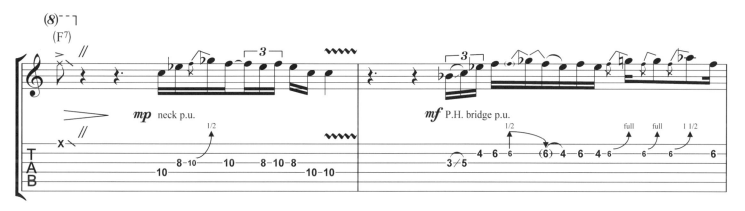

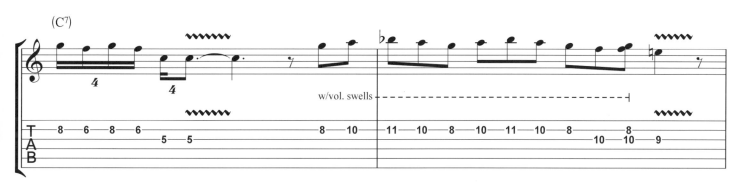

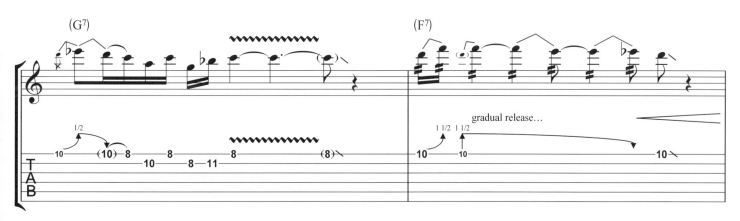

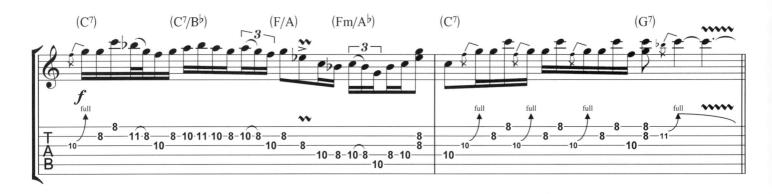

Verse

04:30

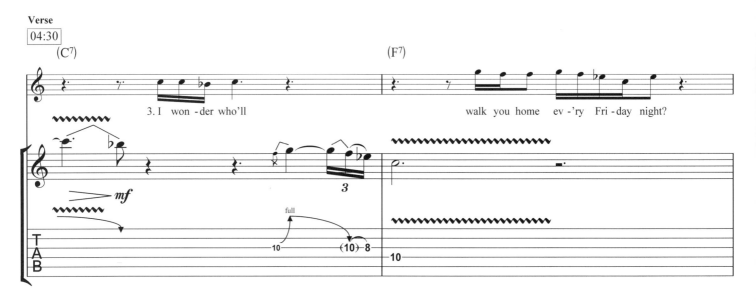

3. I won-der who'll walk you home ev-'ry Fri-day night?

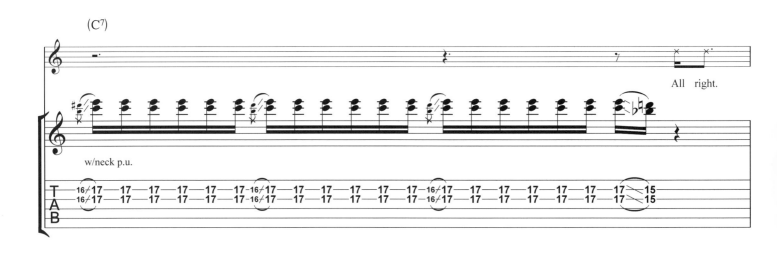

w/neck p.u.

All right.

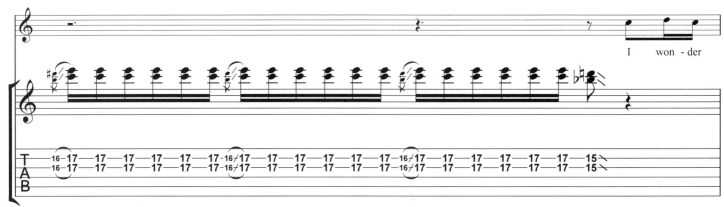

I won-der

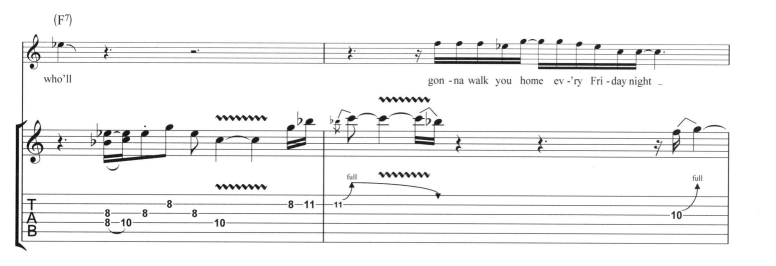

who'll

gon -na walk you home ev -'ry Fri -day night _

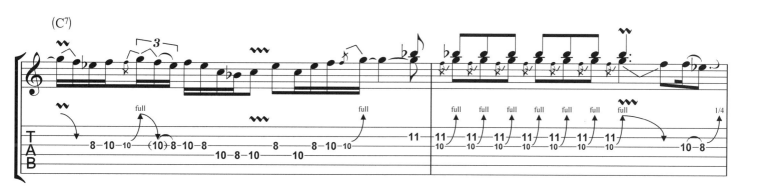

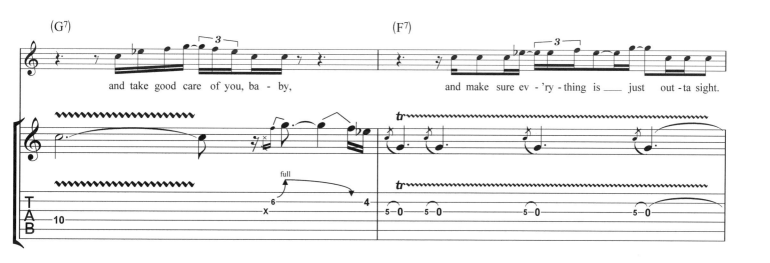

and take good care of you, ba - by,

and make sure ev -'ry-thing is ___ just out -ta sight.

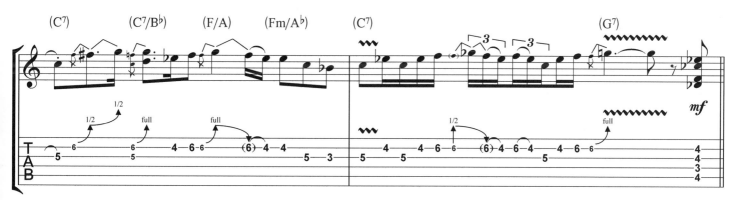

Piano Solo

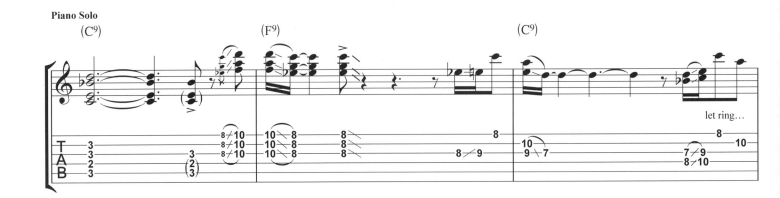

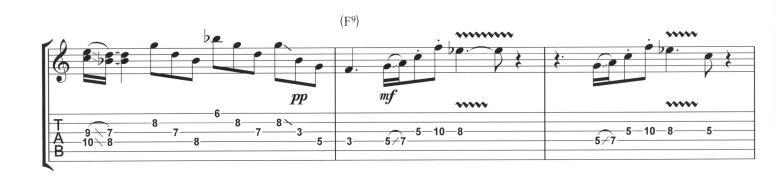

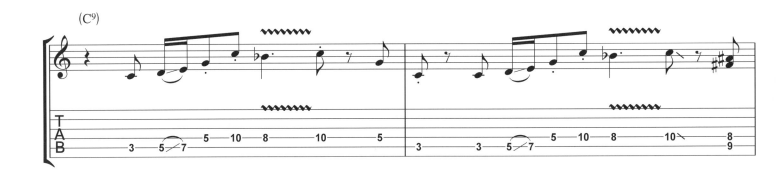

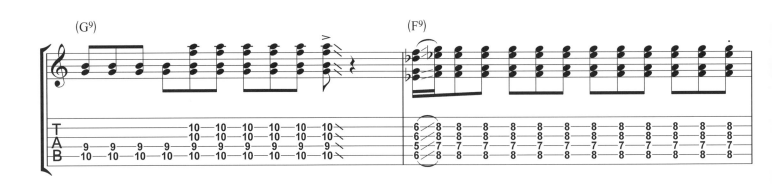

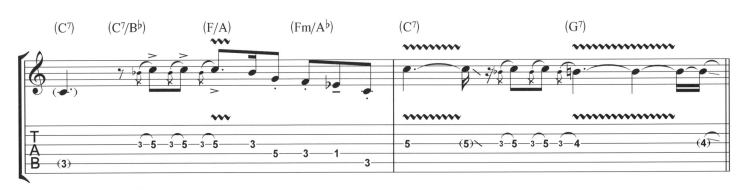

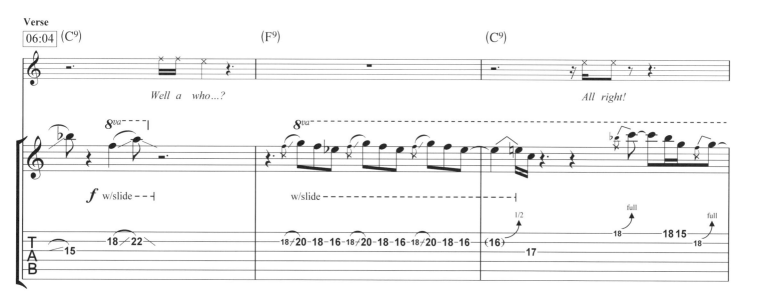

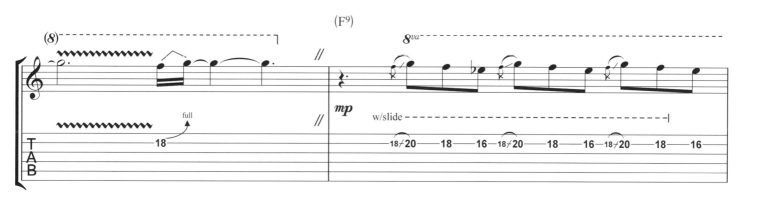

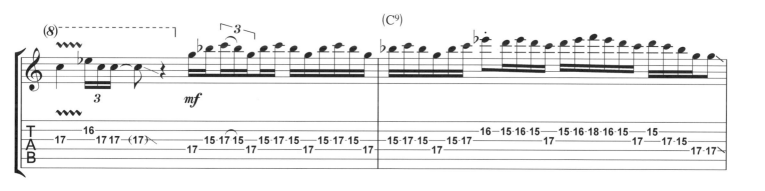

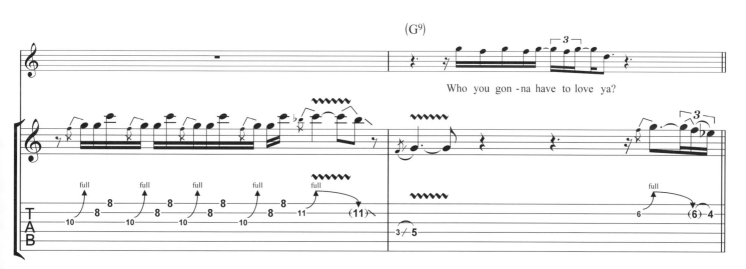

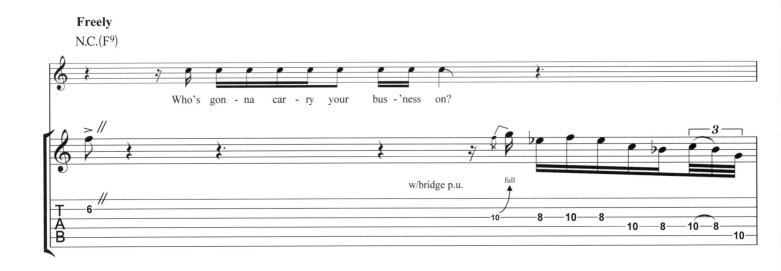

Freely

Who's gon - na car - ry your bus -'ness on?

w/bridge p.u.

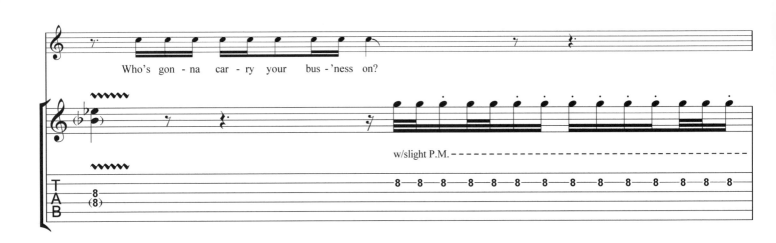

Who's gon - na car - ry your bus -'ness on?

w/slight P.M.

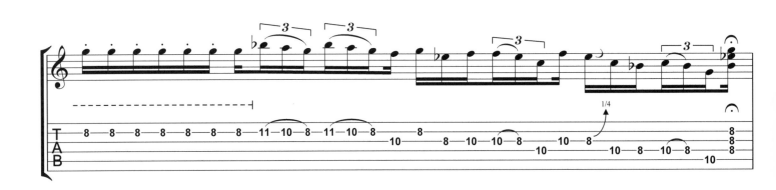

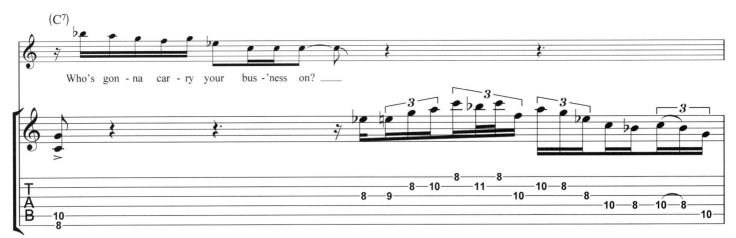

Who's gon - na car - ry your bus -'ness on? ____

54

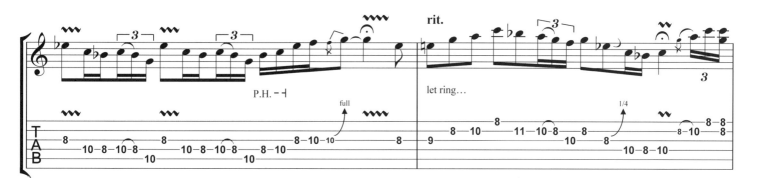

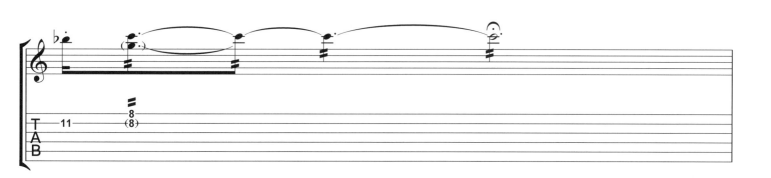

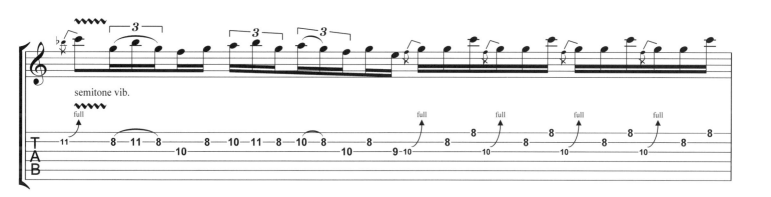

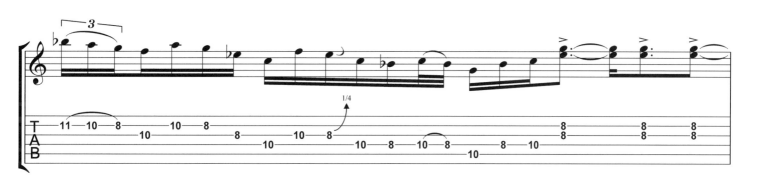

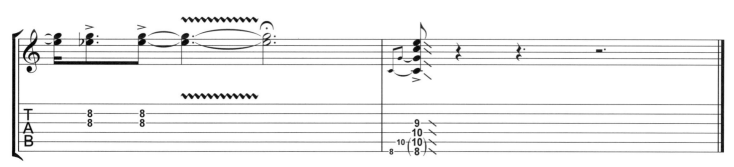

TATTOO'D LADY

Words & Music by Rory Gallagher

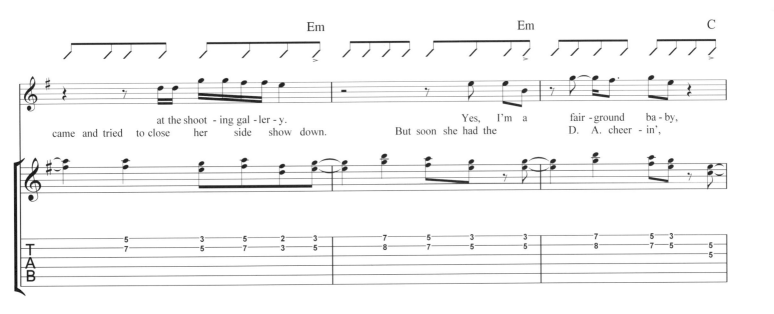

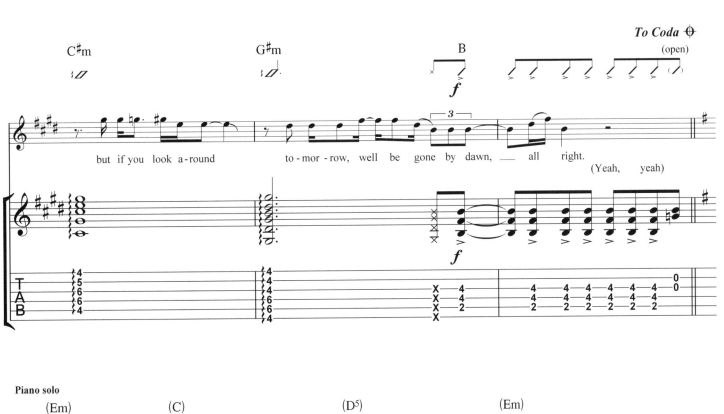

but if you look a-round   to-mor-row, well be gone by dawn, ___ all right.

(Yeah,   yeah)

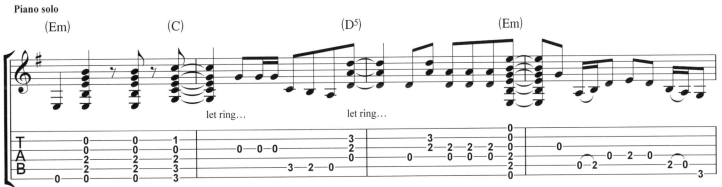

Piano solo

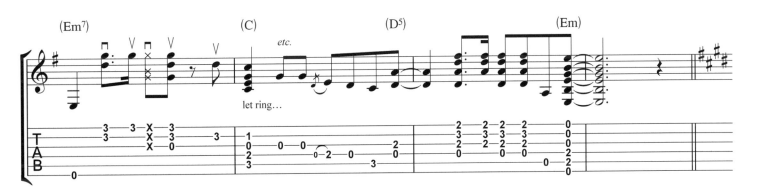

Solo

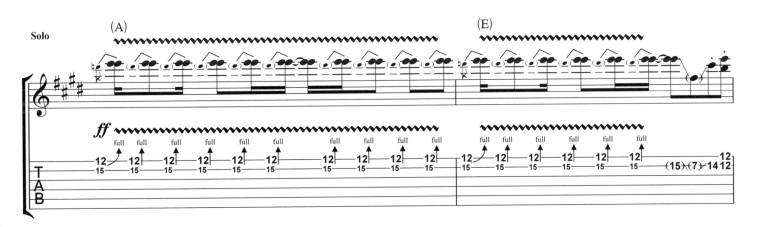

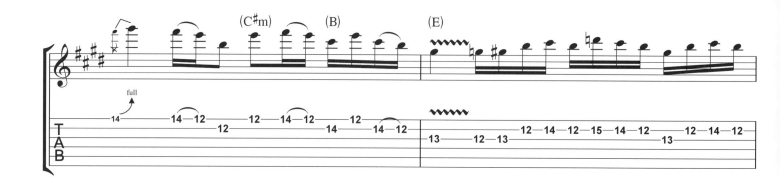

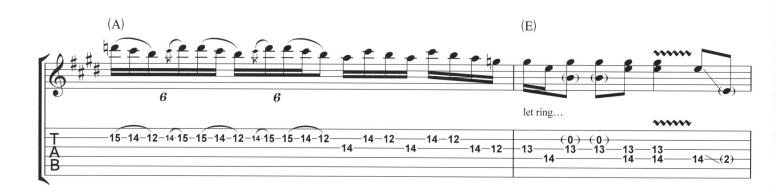

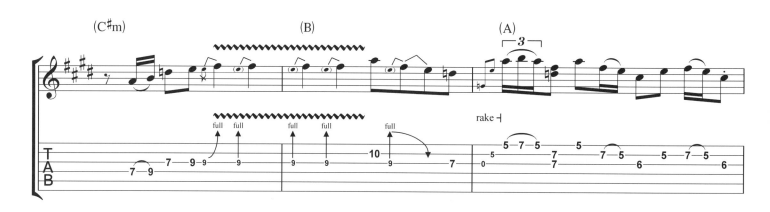

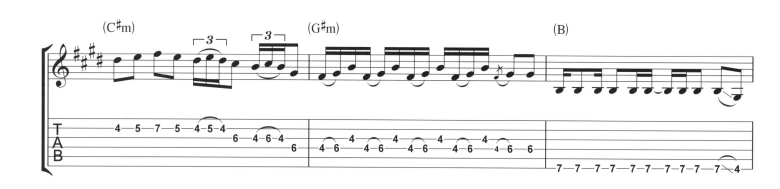

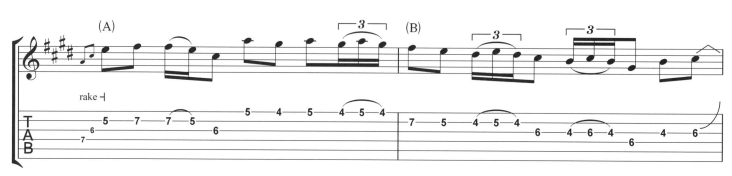

Solo

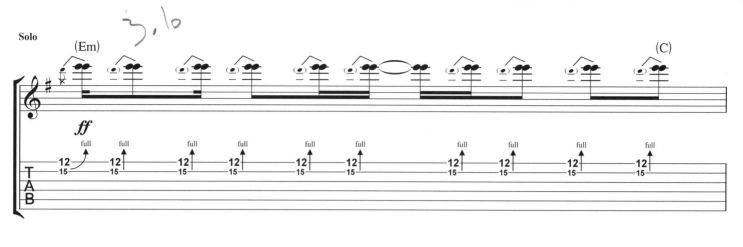

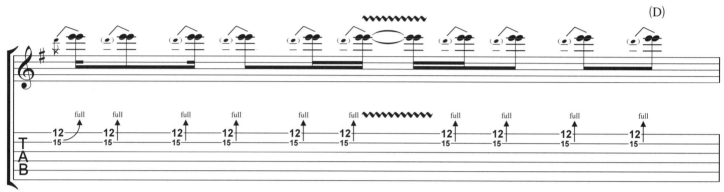

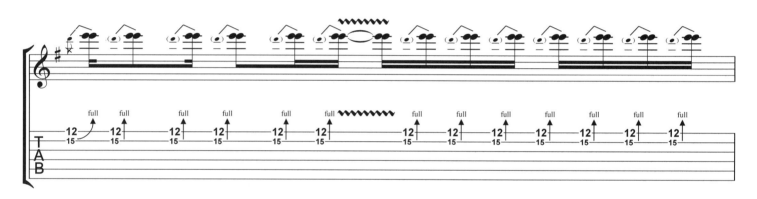

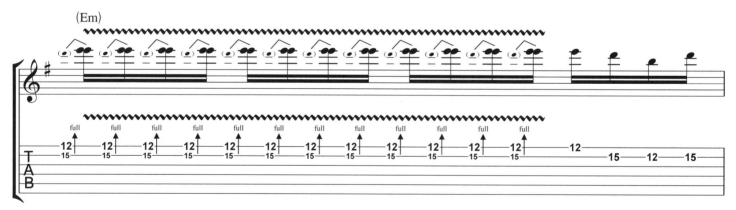

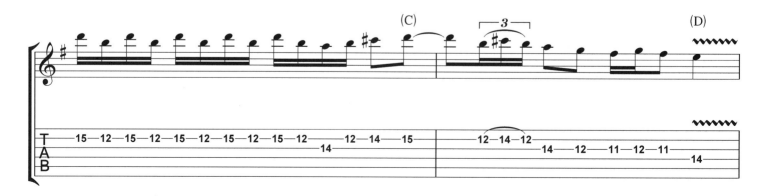

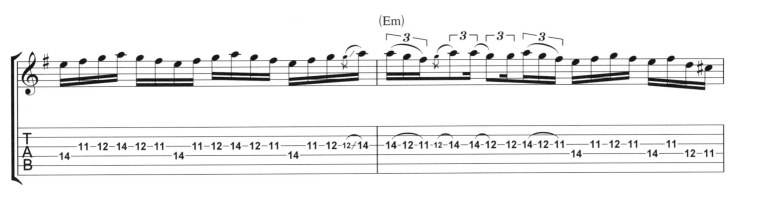

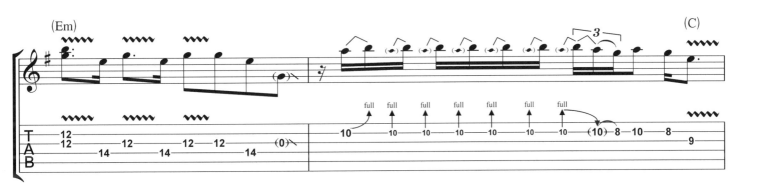

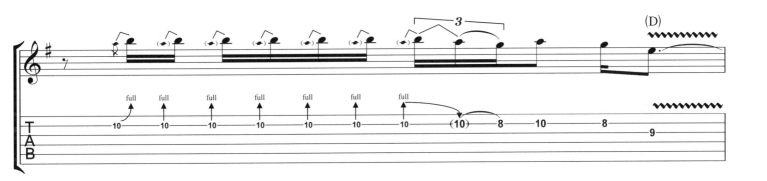

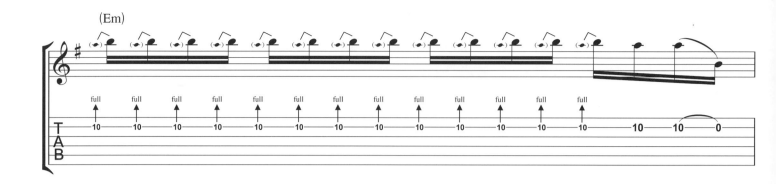

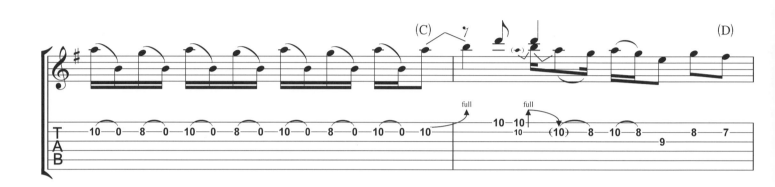

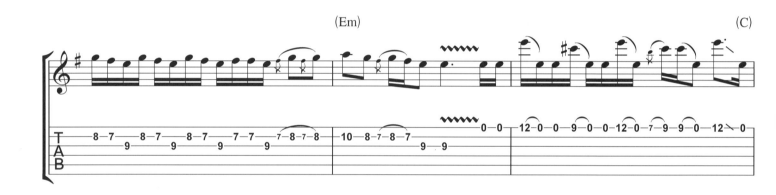

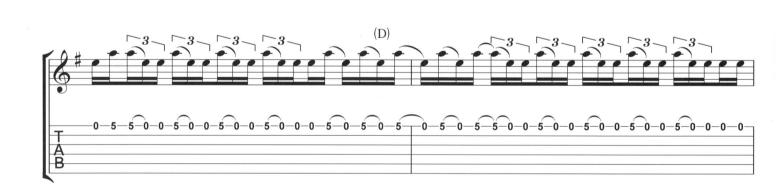

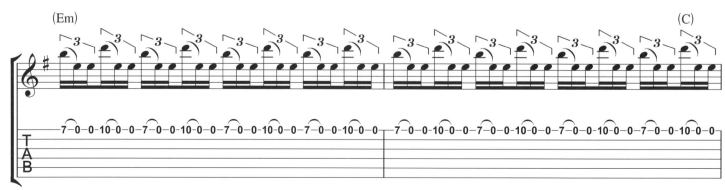

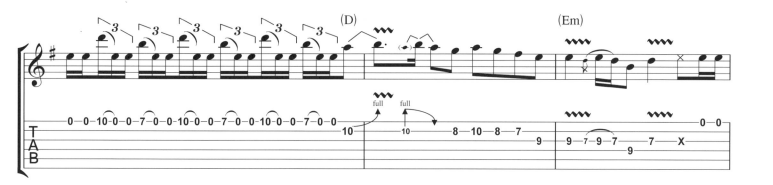

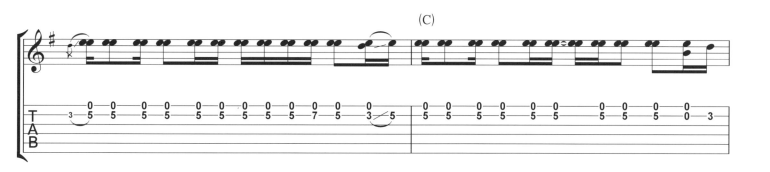

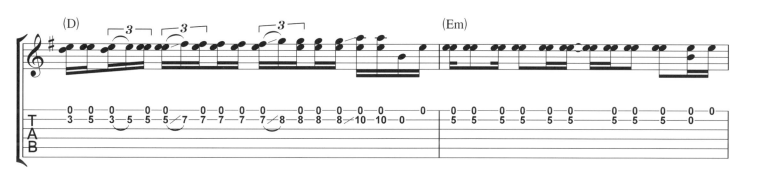

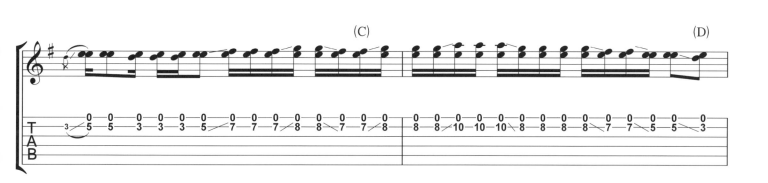

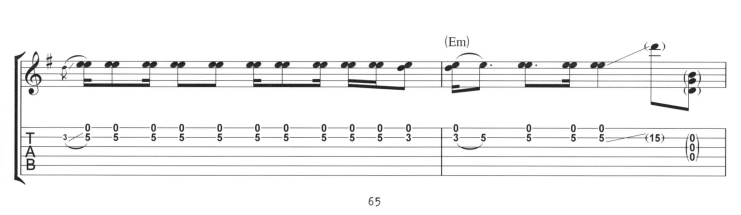

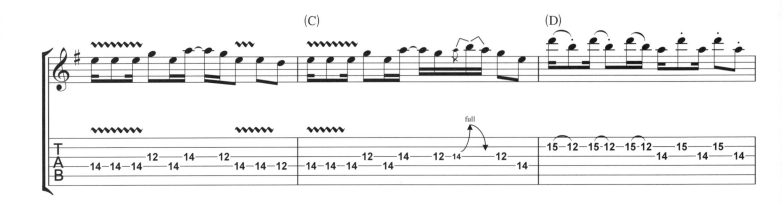

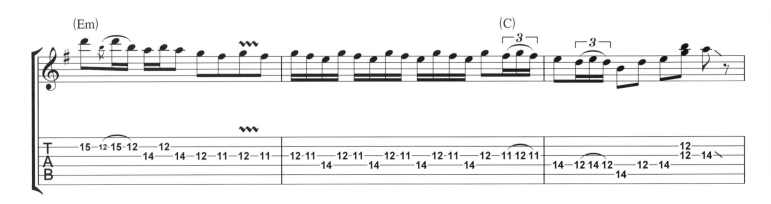

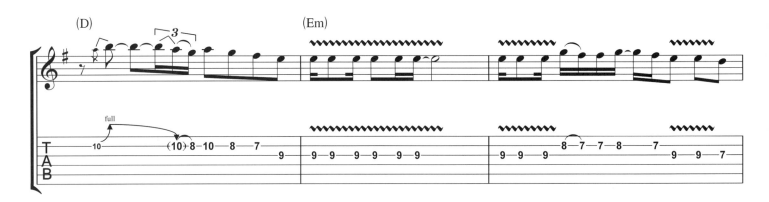

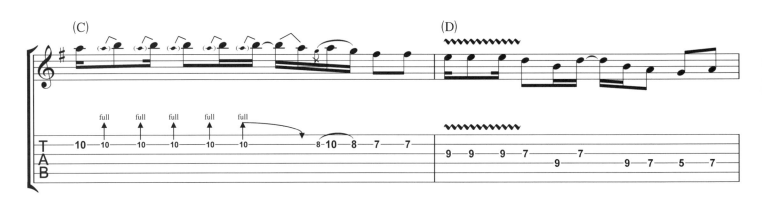

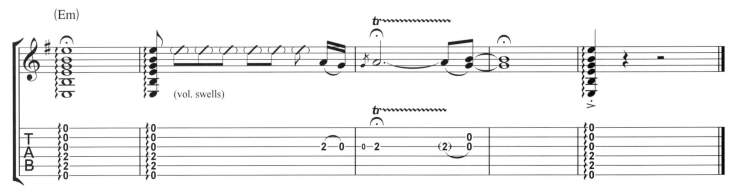

WALK ON HOT COALS

Words & Music by Rory Gallagher

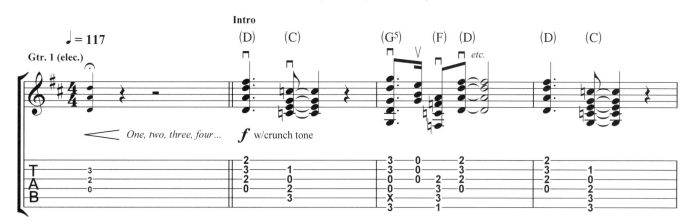

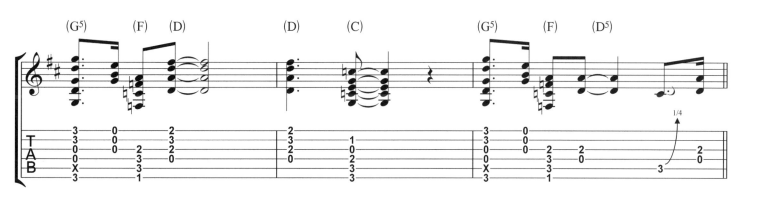

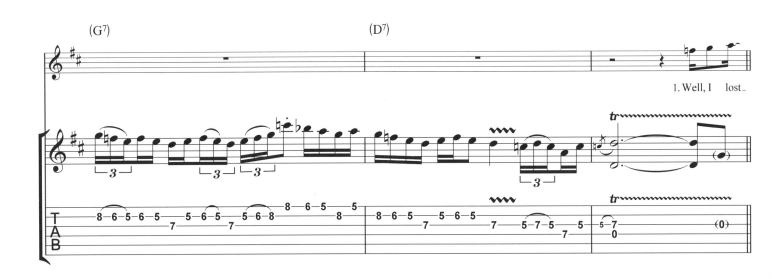

1. Well, I lost

Verse

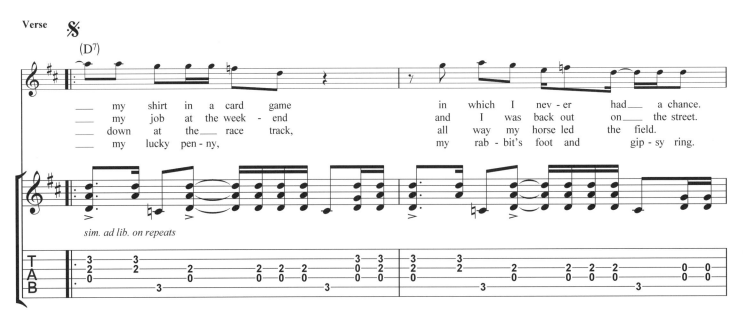

___ my shirt in a card game   in which I nev - er   had ___ a chance.
___ my job at the week - end   and I was back out   on ___ the street.
___ down at the ___ race track,   all way my horse led   the field.
___ my lucky pen - ny,   my rab - bit's foot and   gip - sy ring.

sim. ad lib. on repeats

68

Well, I lost__
Well, I lost__
Spent it all__
Throw a - way__

(G⁷)

__ my shirt in a card game   in which I ne - ver had__ a chance.
__ my job at the week - end,   I was back out on__ the street.
__ down on the__ race - track   all the way my horse led__ the field.
__ my lucky pen - ny,   that was what I just played.

(D⁷)

The
That's no
But it
Not gon - na

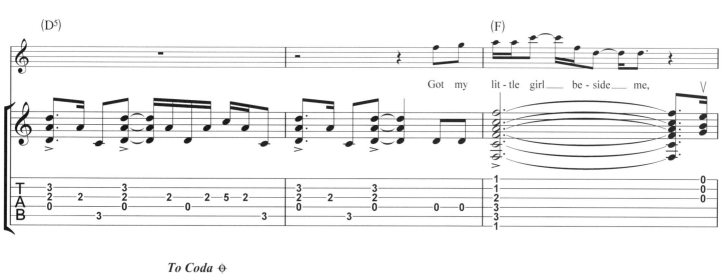

Got my lit-tle girl be-side me,

To Coda ⊕

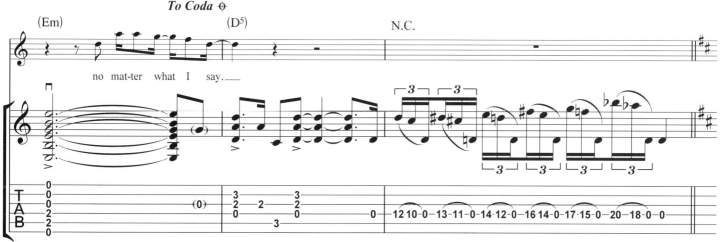

no mat-ter what I say.

N.C.

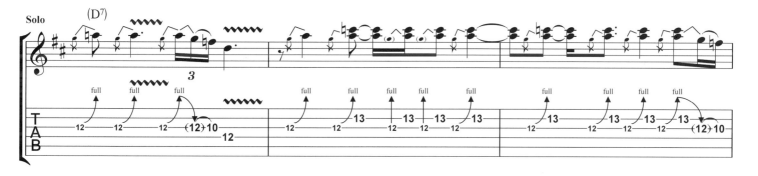

Solo

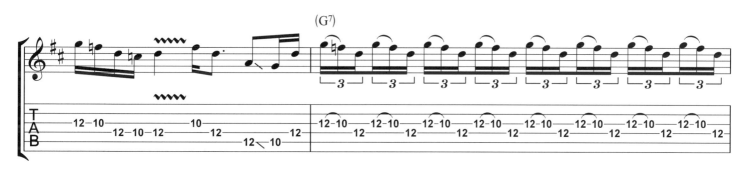

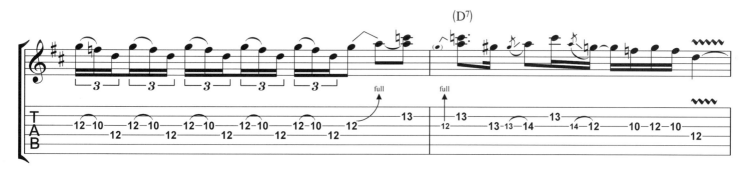

71

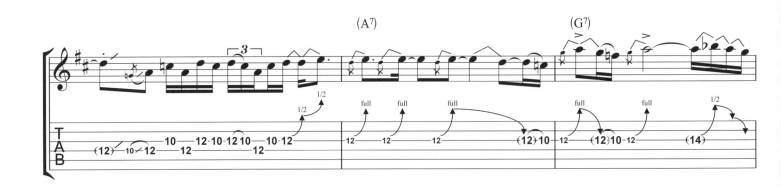

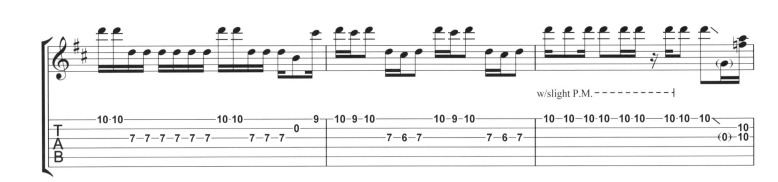

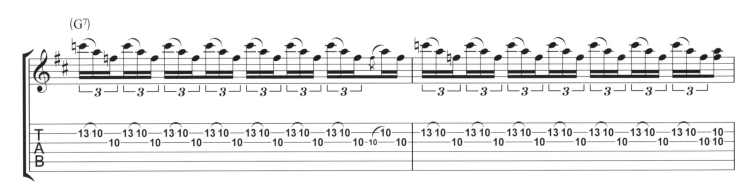

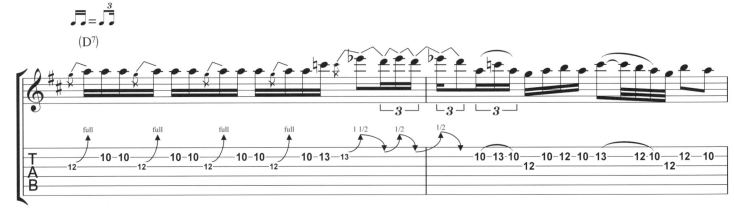

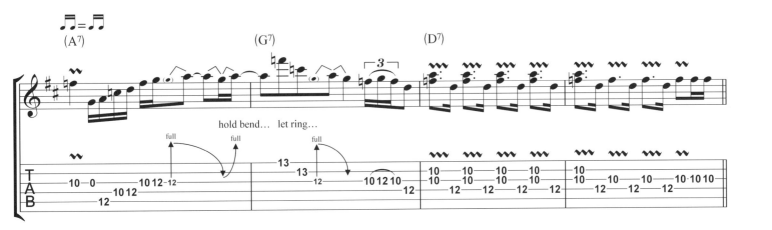

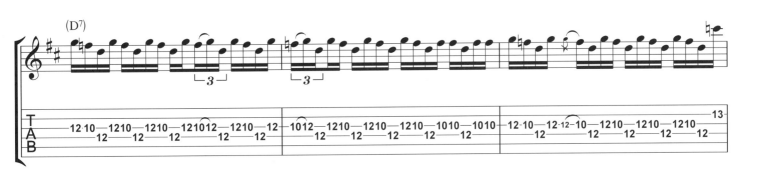

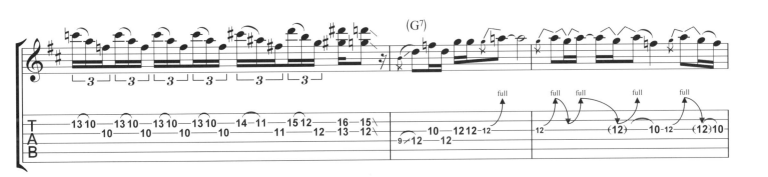

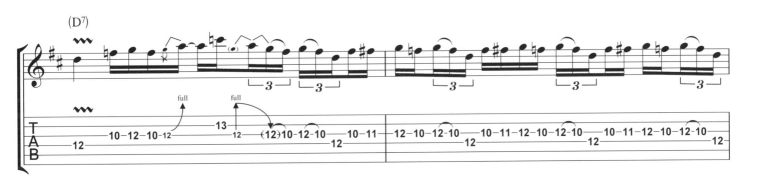

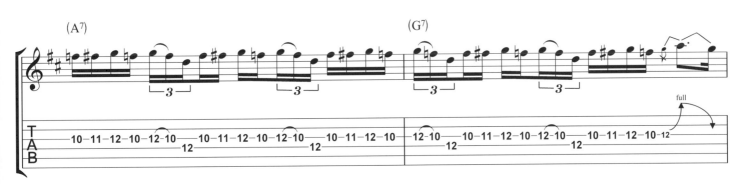

3. Gon - na throw

Coda

Yes, I walk on hot coals,___

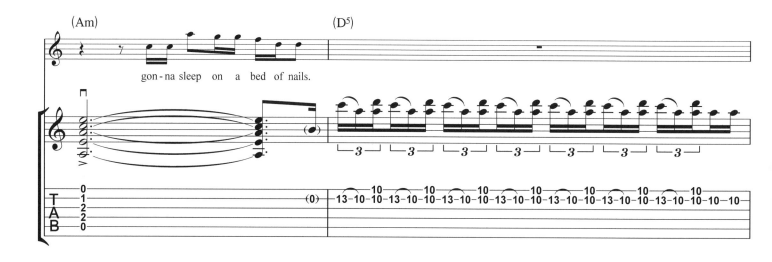

gon - na sleep on a bed of nails.

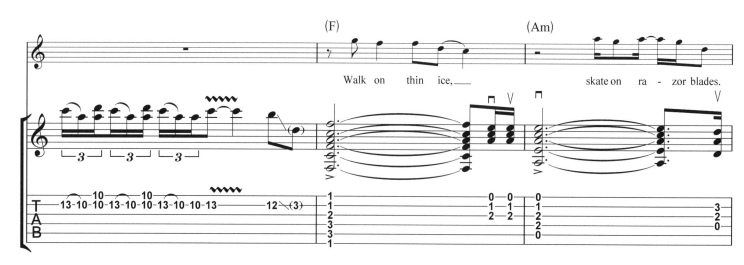

Walk on thin ice,___ skate on ra - zor blades.

Got my lit - tle girl___ be - side___ me,

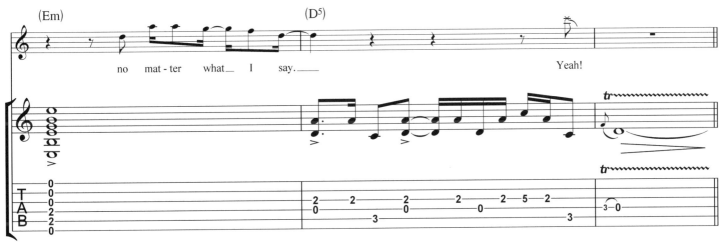

no mat - ter what___ I say.___ Yeah!

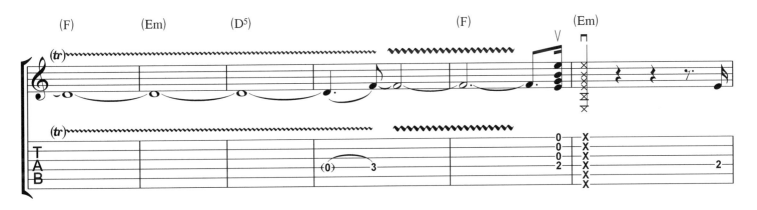

w/variable P.M.

75

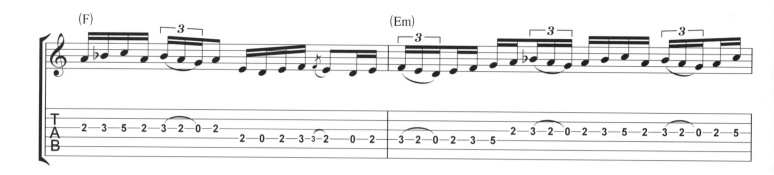

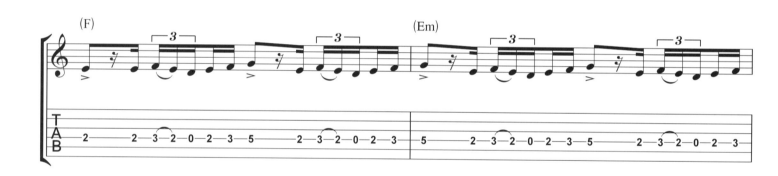

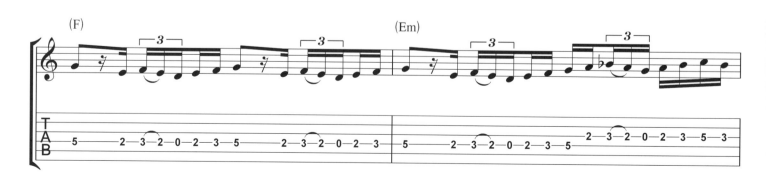

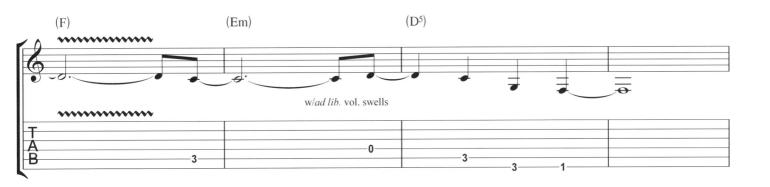

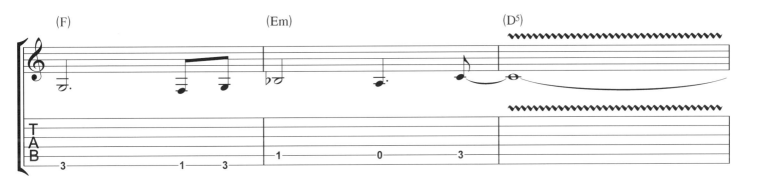

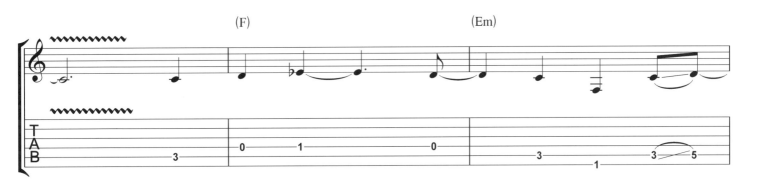

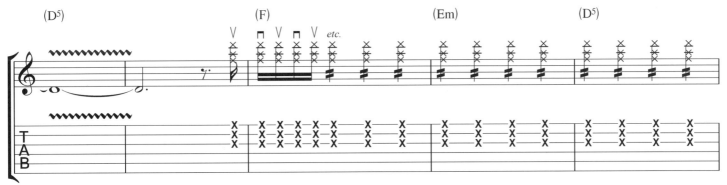

77

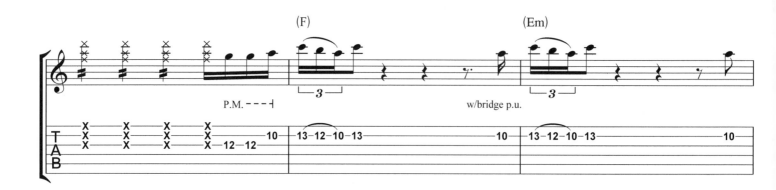

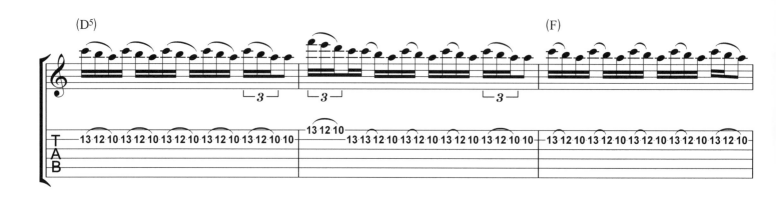

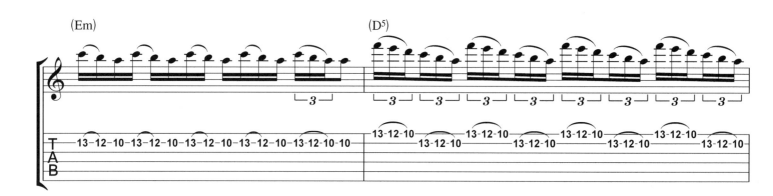

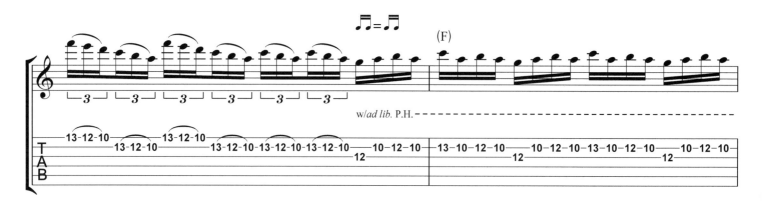

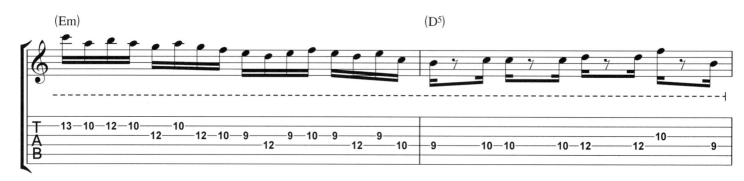

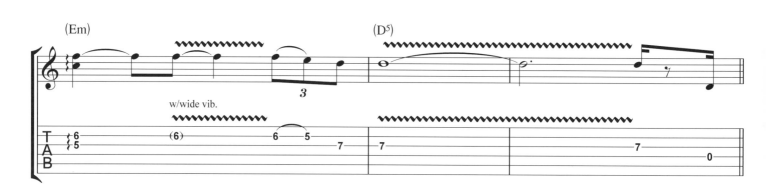

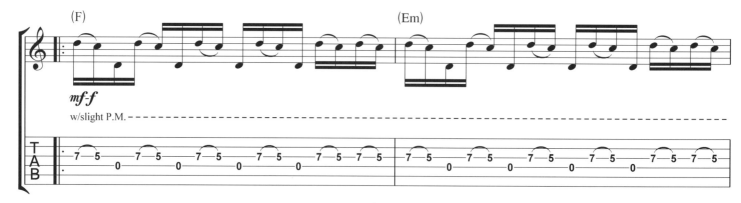

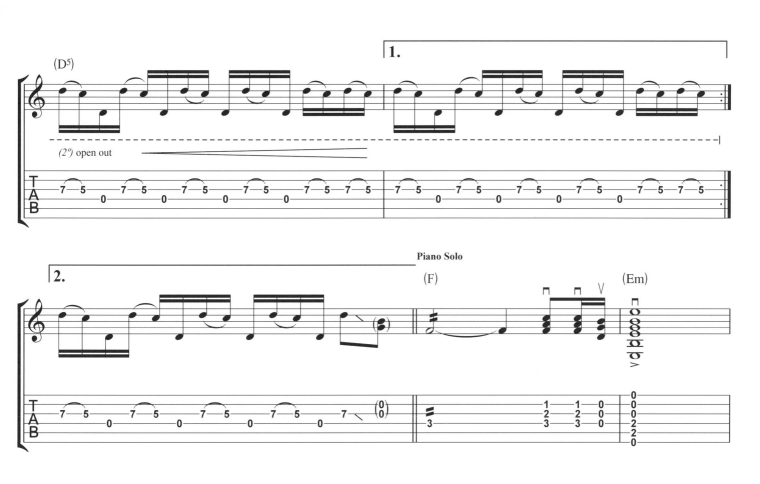

Piano Solo

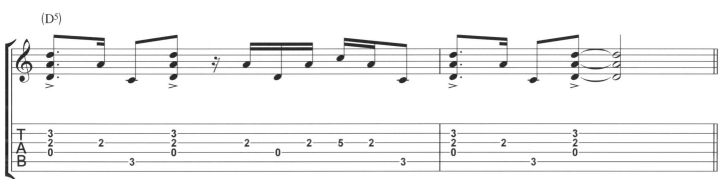

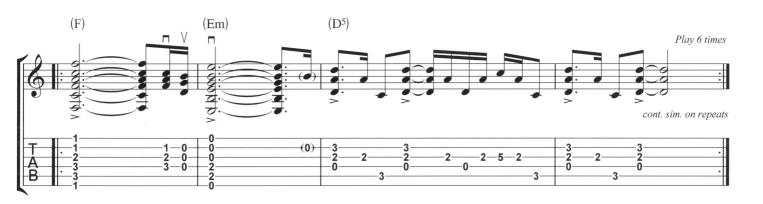

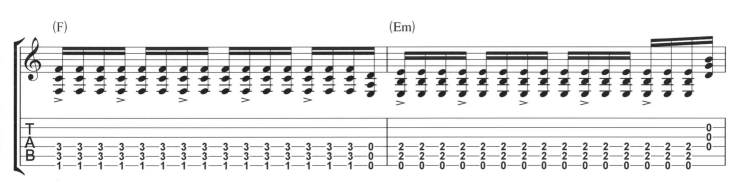

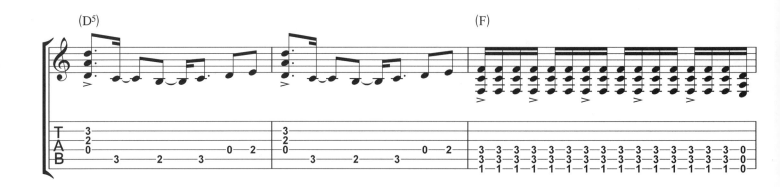

Breakdown

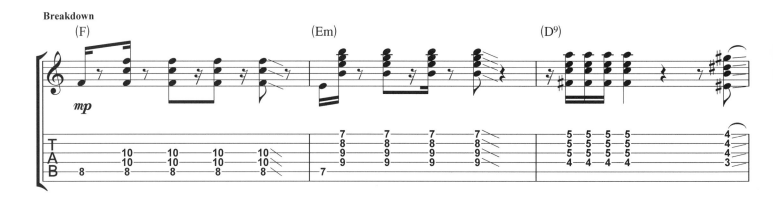

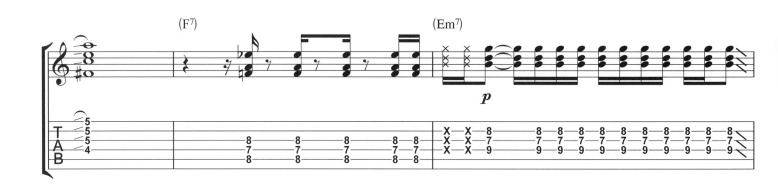

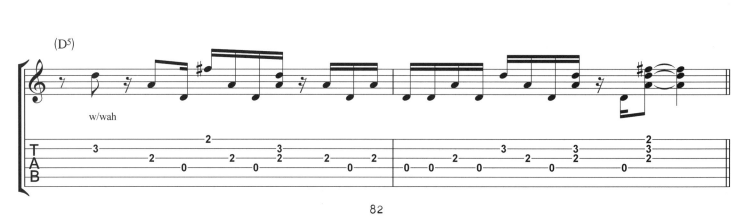

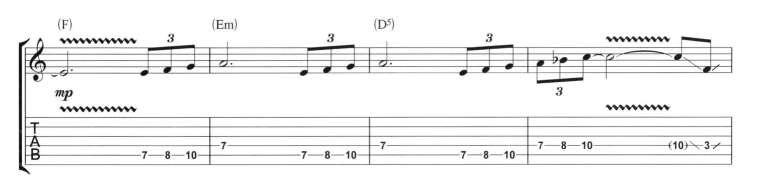

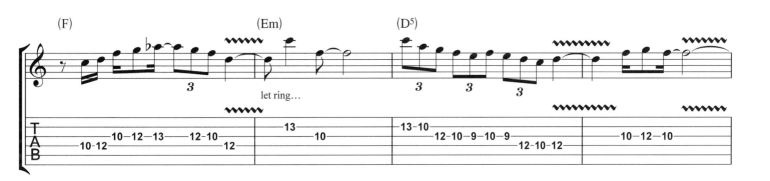

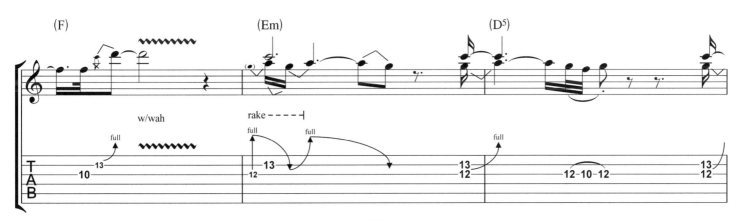

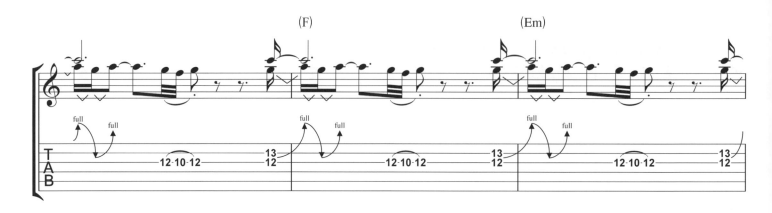
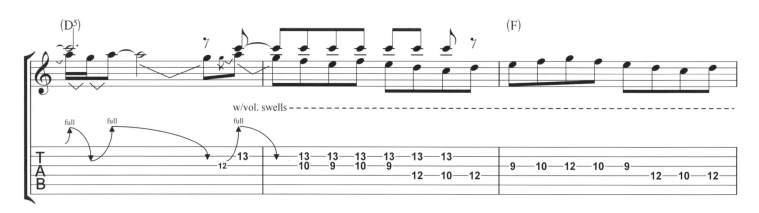
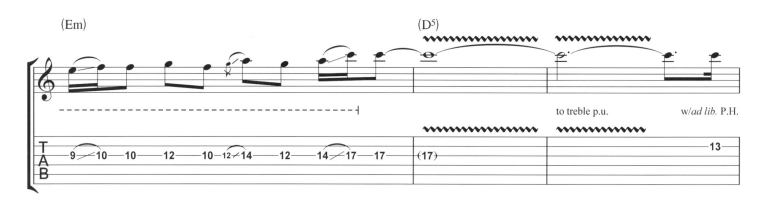
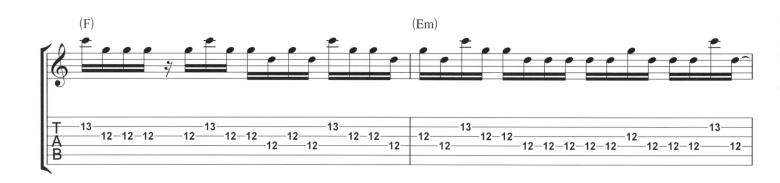
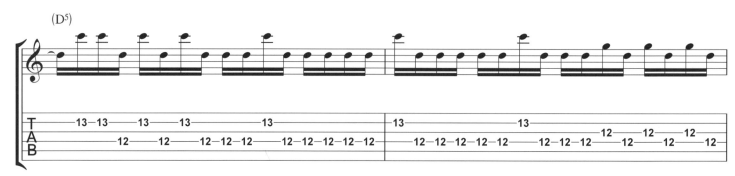

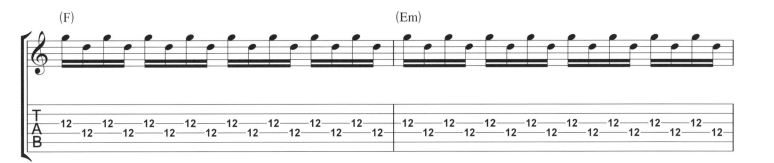

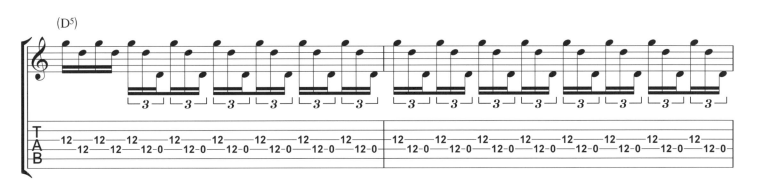

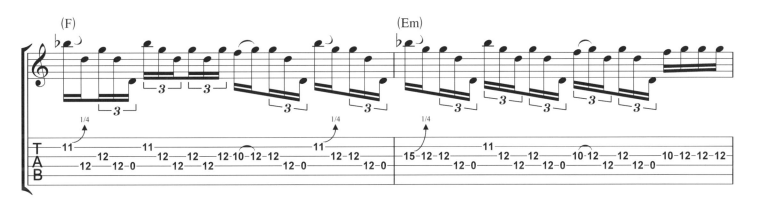

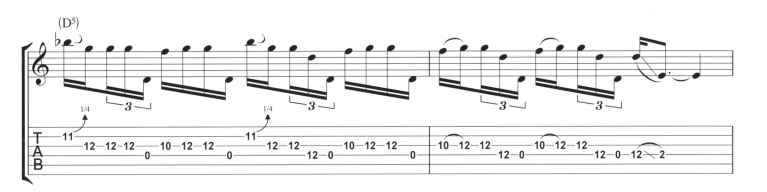

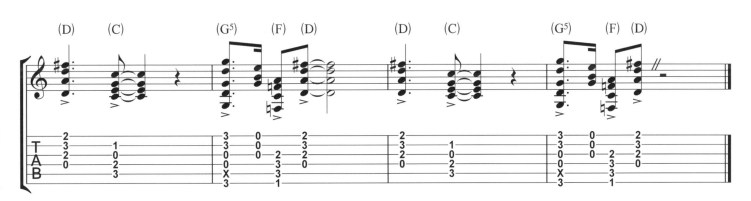

85

LAUNDROMAT

Words & Music by Rory Gallagher

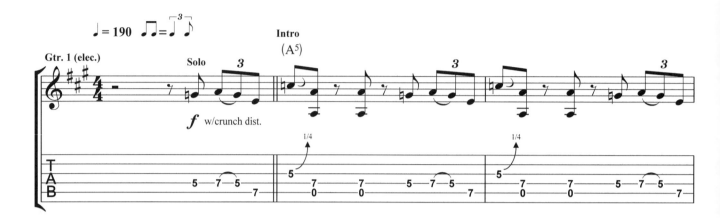

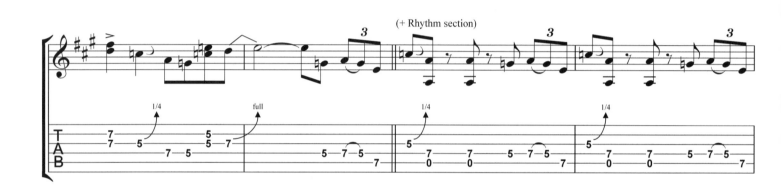

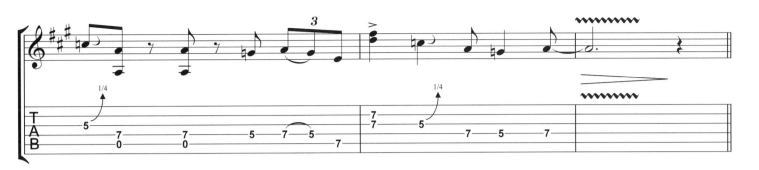

Verse

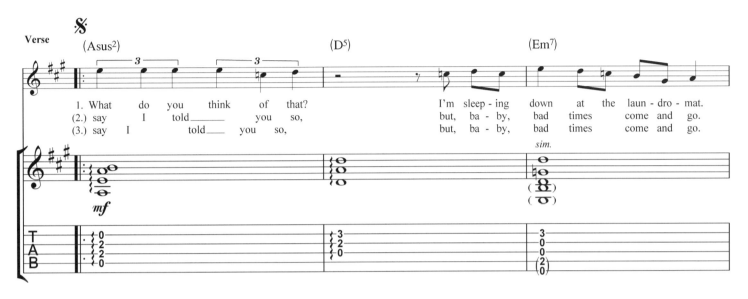

(Asus²)   (D⁵)   (Em⁷)

1. What do you think of that?   I'm sleep - ing down at the laun - dro - mat.
(2.) say I told____ you so,   but, ba - by, bad times come and go.
(3.) say I told____ you so,   but, ba - by, bad times come and go.

sim.

mf

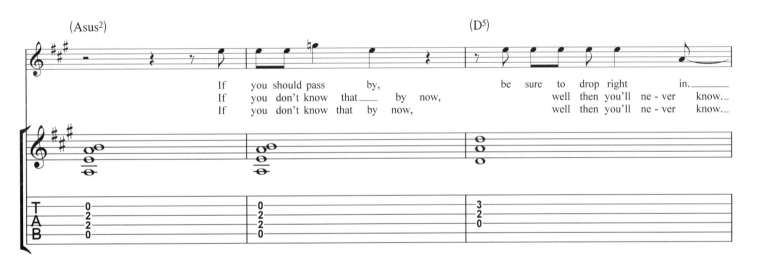

(Asus²)   (D⁵)

If you should pass by,   be sure to drop right in.____
If you don't know that____ by now,   well then you'll ne - ver know.____
If you don't know that by now,   well then you'll ne - ver know.____

(A)

f Fig. 1 -
(2º, 3º) Gtr. 1 plays Fig. 2

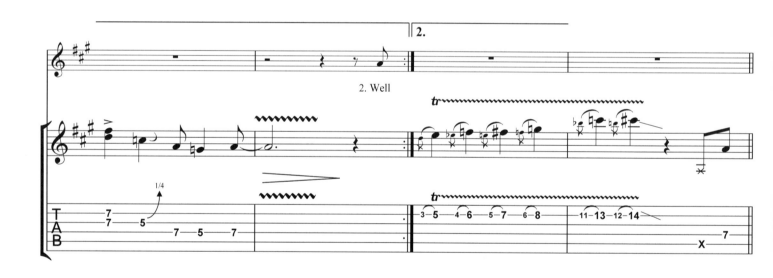

90

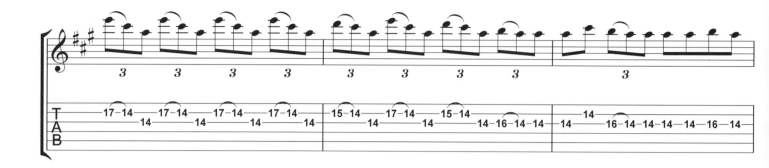

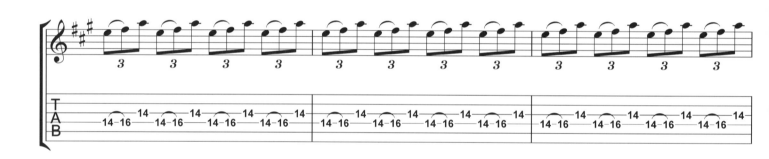

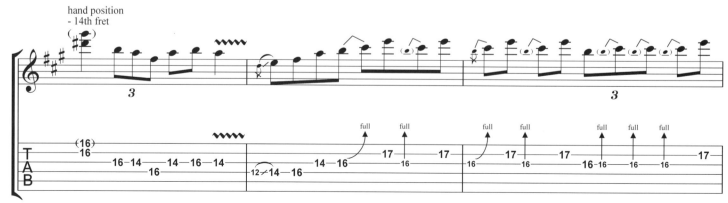

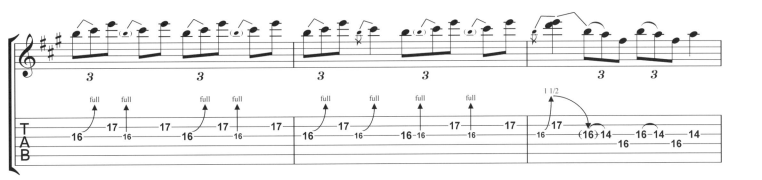

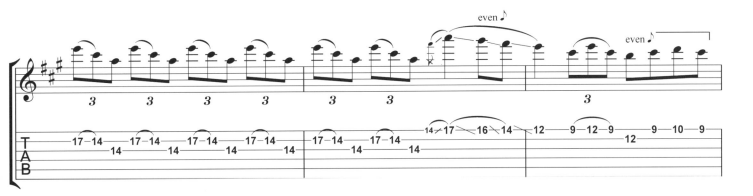

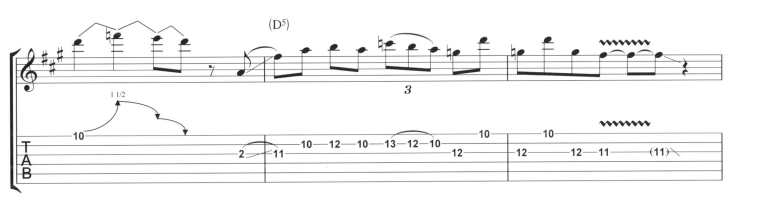

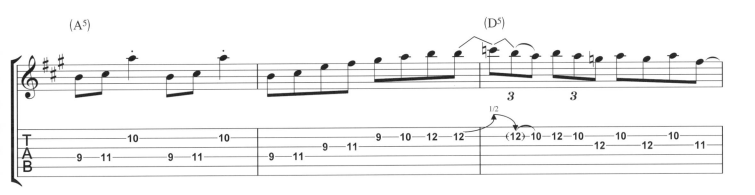

94

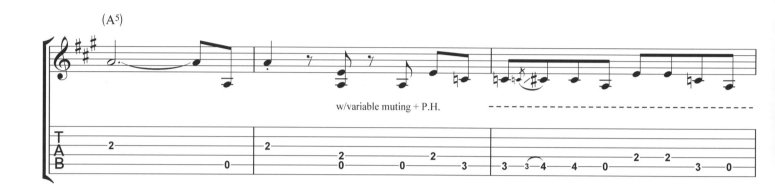

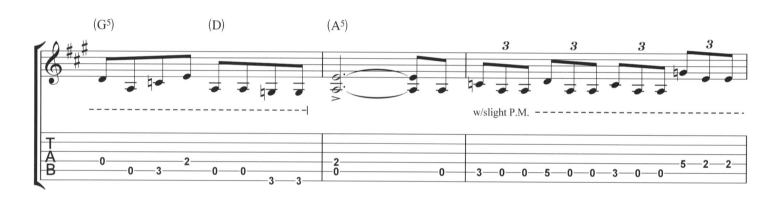

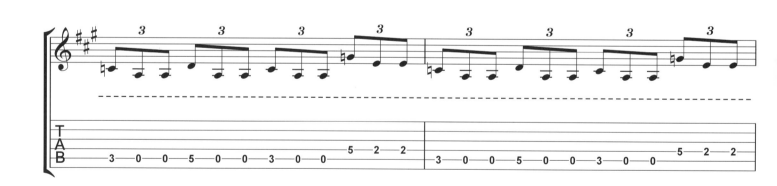

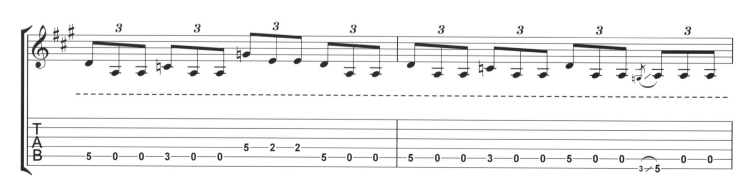

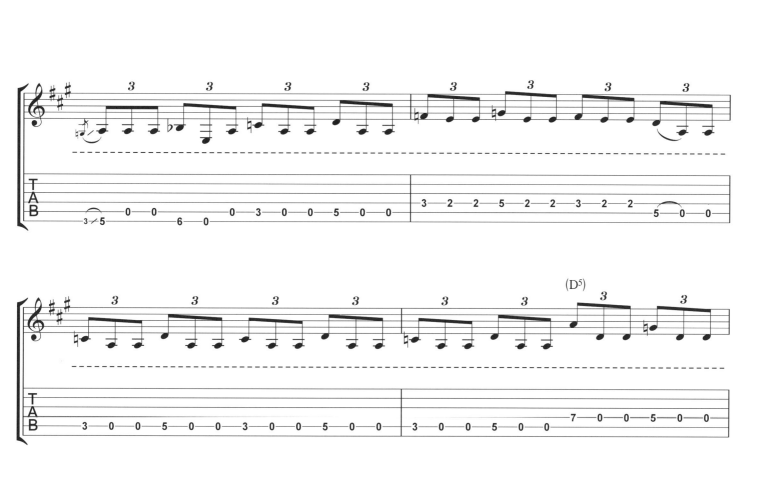

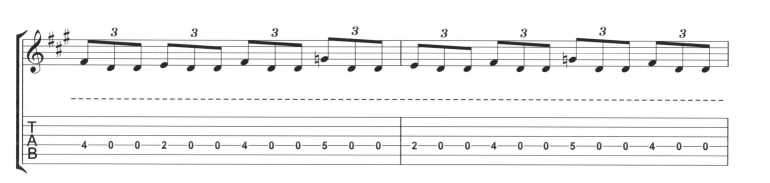

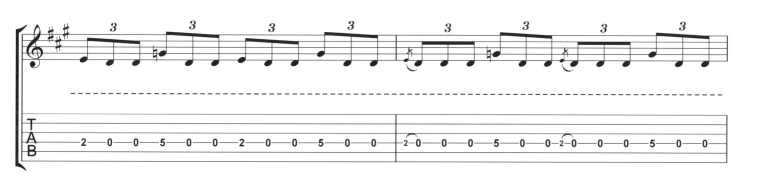

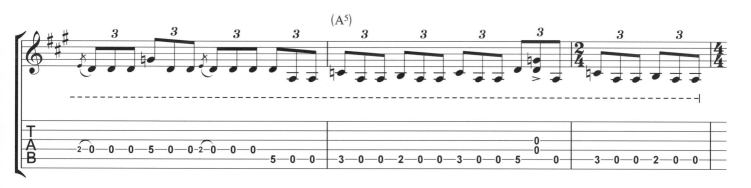

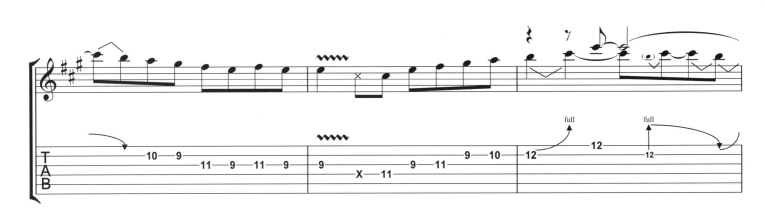

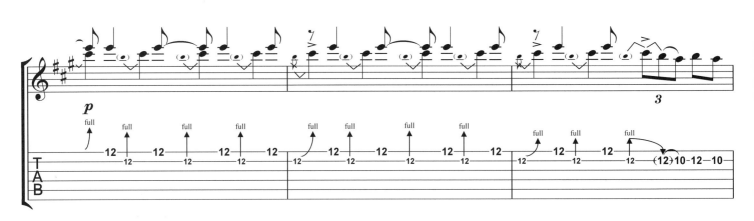

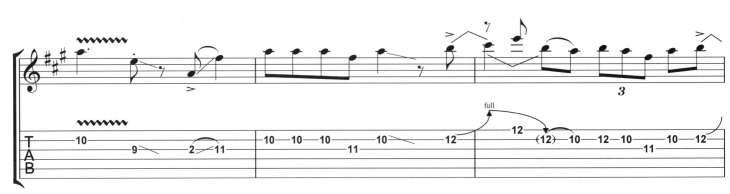

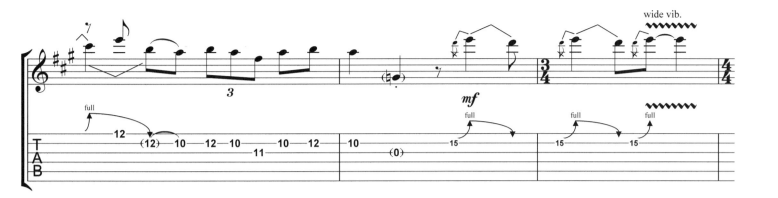

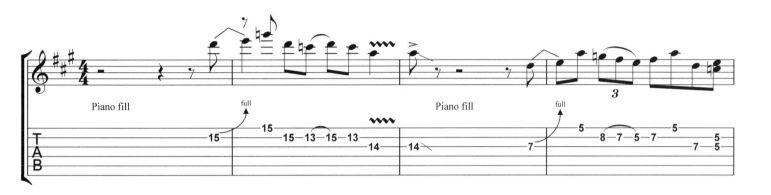

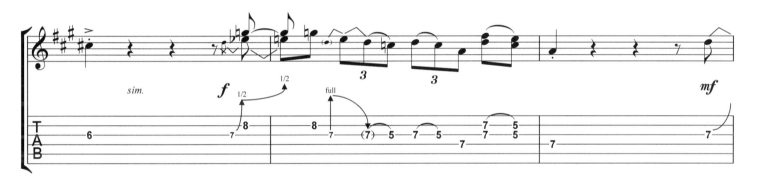

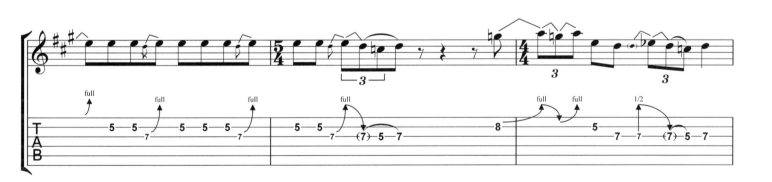

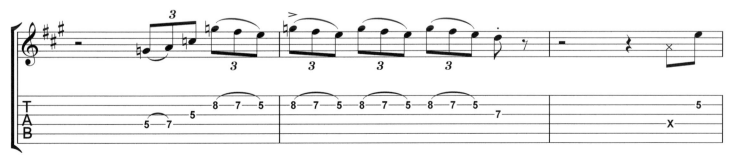

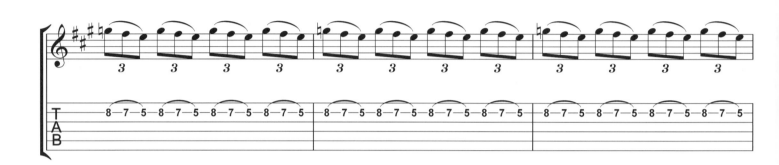

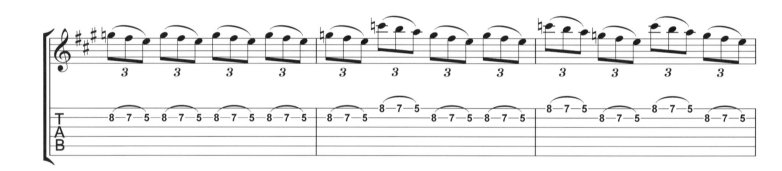

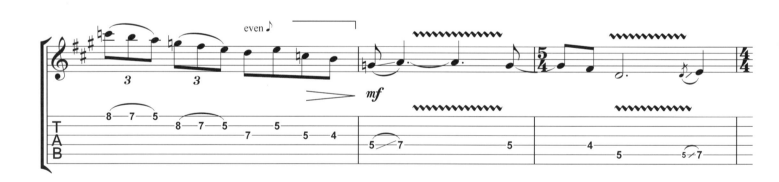

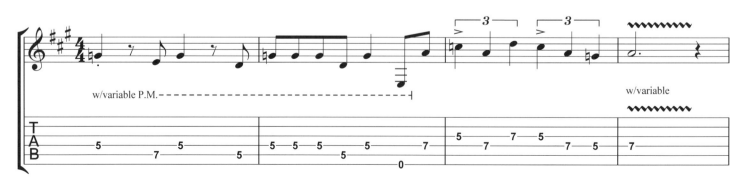

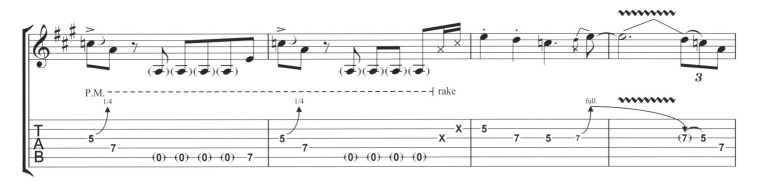

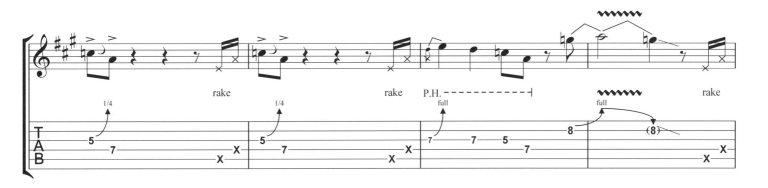

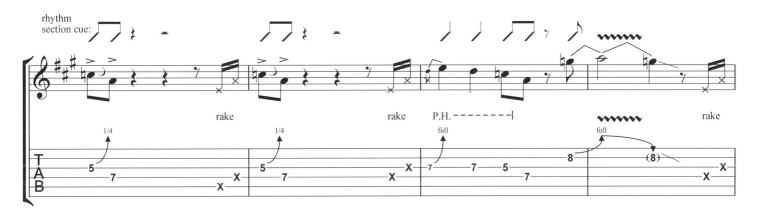

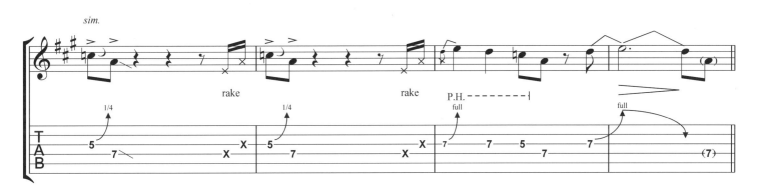

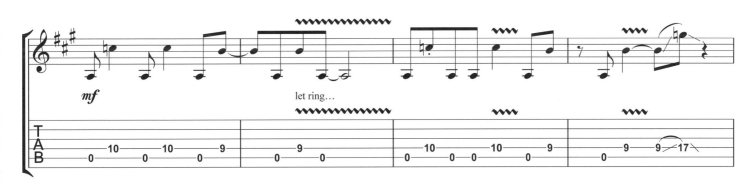

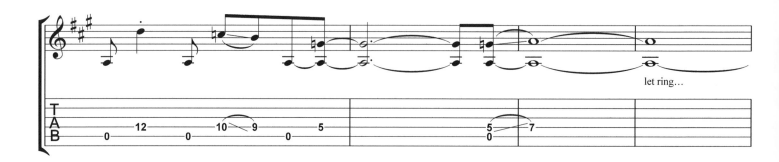
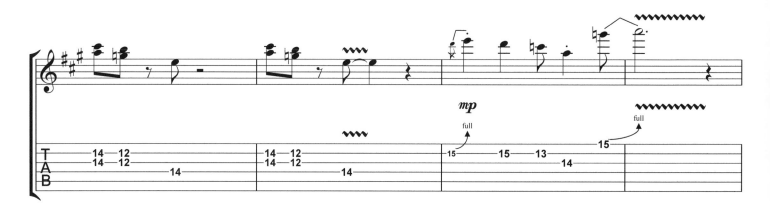
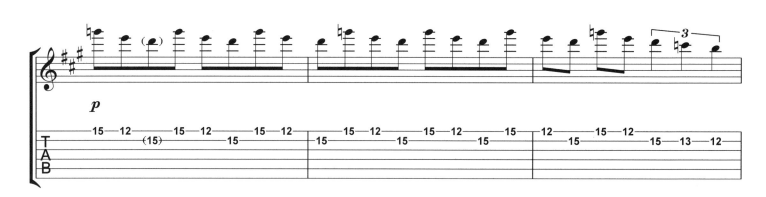
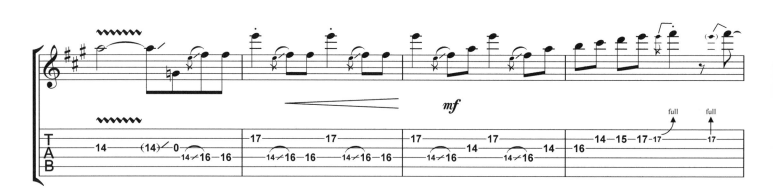
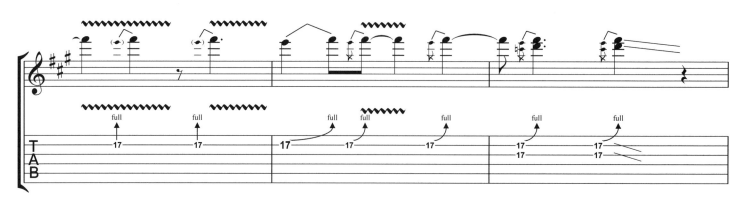

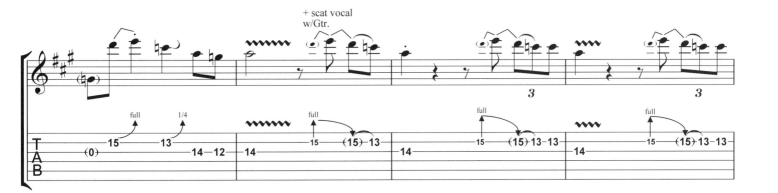

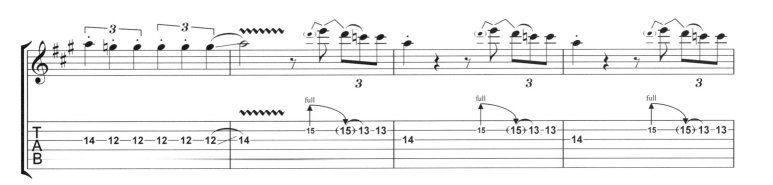

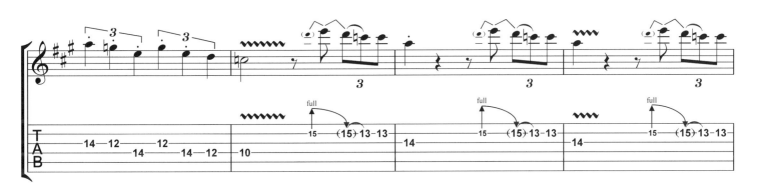

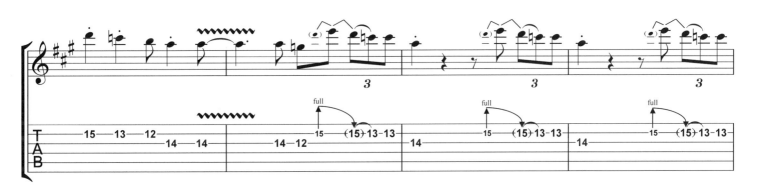

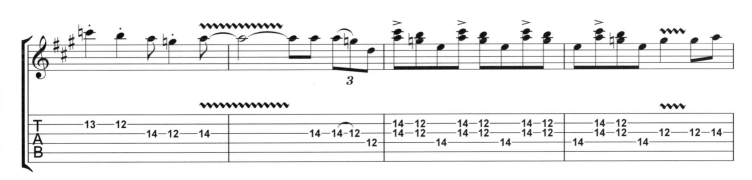

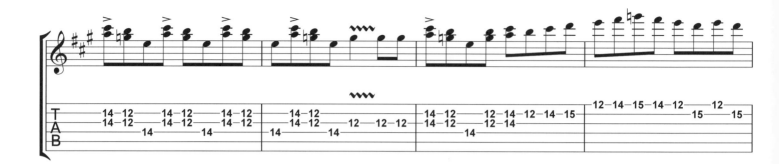

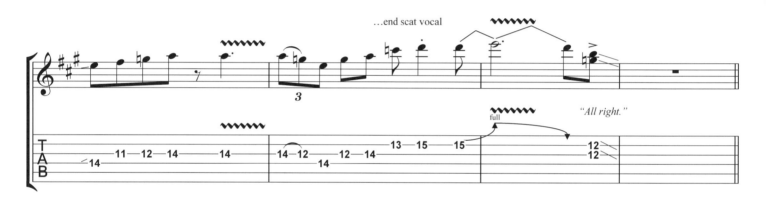

Outro

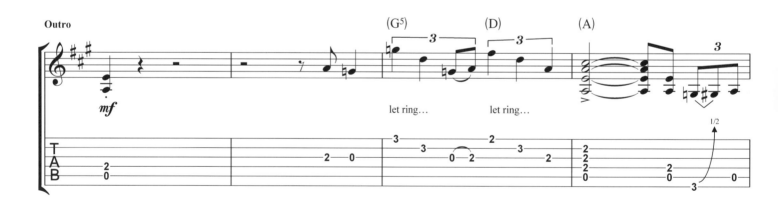

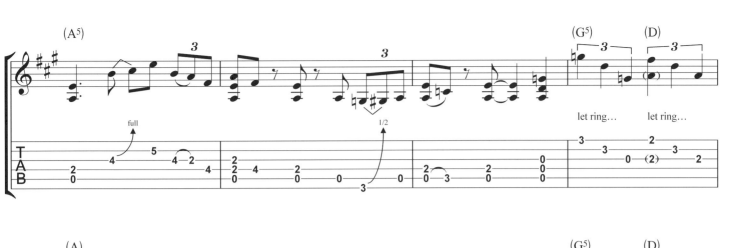

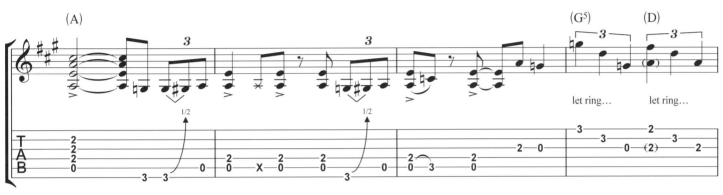

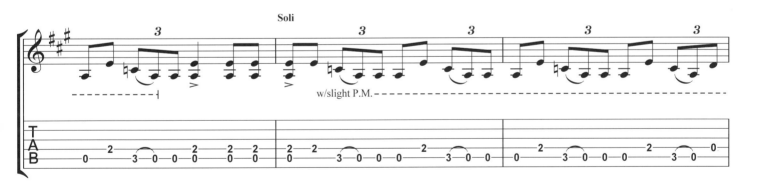

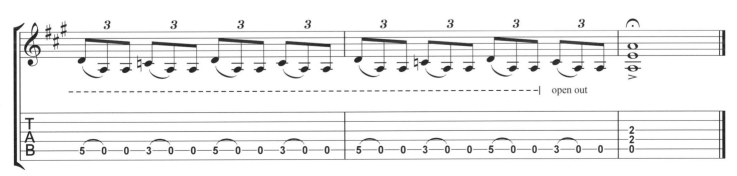

A MILLION MILES AWAY

Words & Music by Rory Gallagher

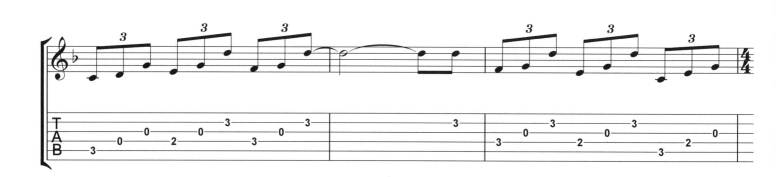

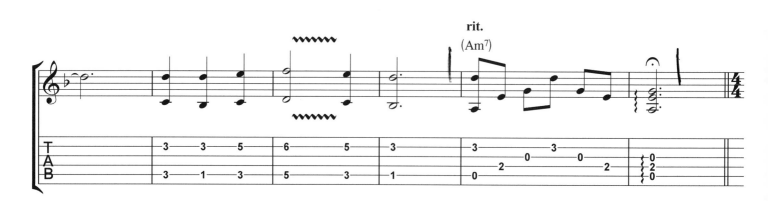

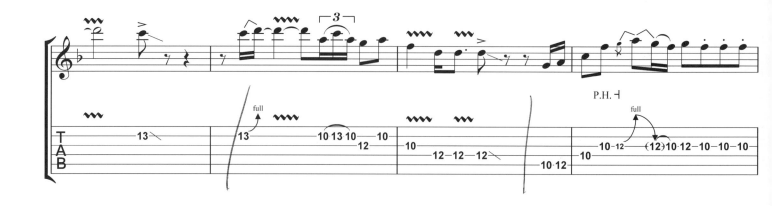

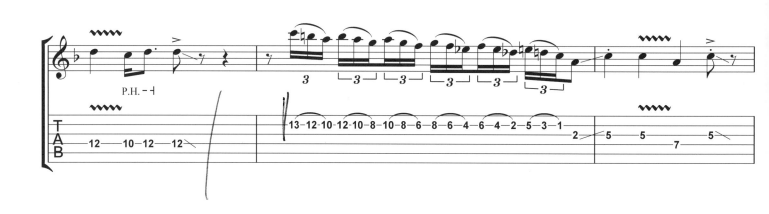

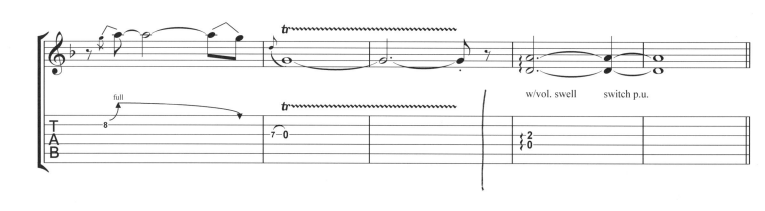

Verse

(D⁵) 1.22   (F⁵)

1. This ho-tel bar___ is full of peo-ple.

Lyrics:
The pi - a - no man___ is real - ly layin' it down.

The old___ bar - ten - der is as high___ as a steep - le.

So why___ to - night___ should I wear a frown?___

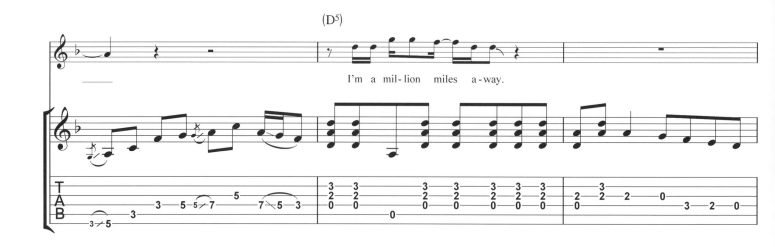

(D⁵)

I'm a mil-lion miles a-way.

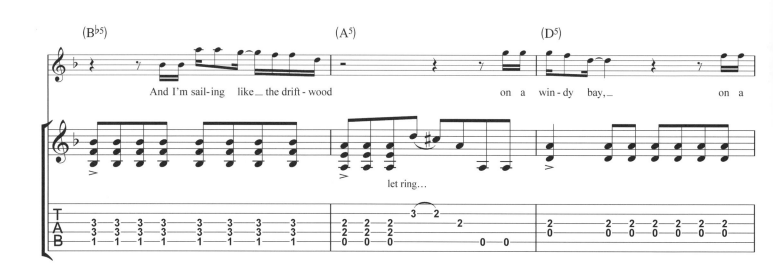

(B♭⁵)

And I'm sail-ing like ___ the drift-wood

(A⁵)

on a win-dy bay, ___

(D⁵)

on a

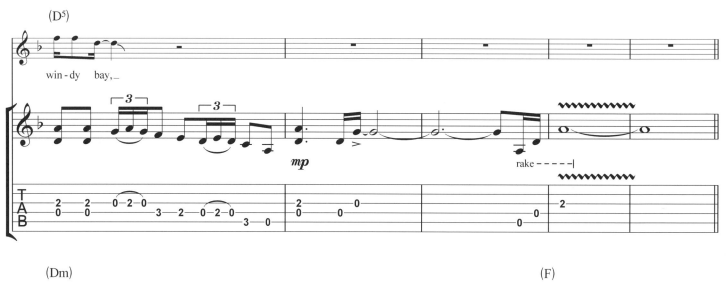

(D⁵)

win-dy bay, ___

let ring…

mp

rake -----|

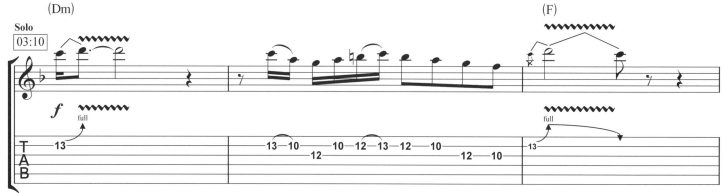

(Dm)

Solo
03:10

(F)

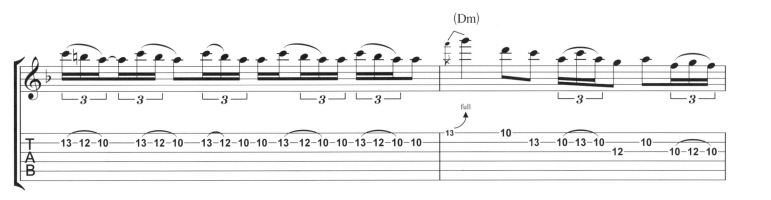

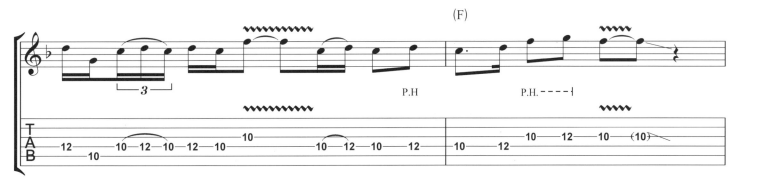

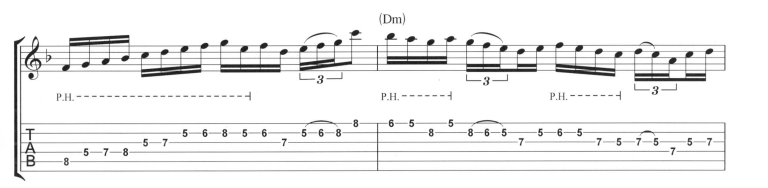

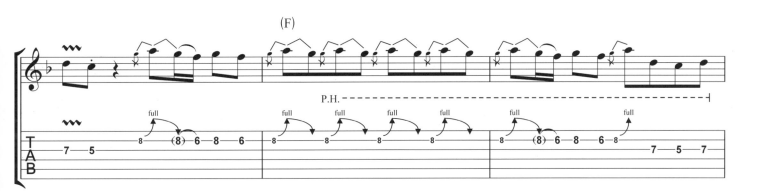

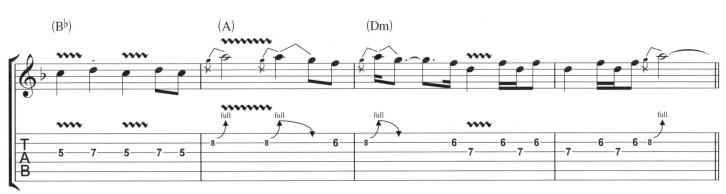

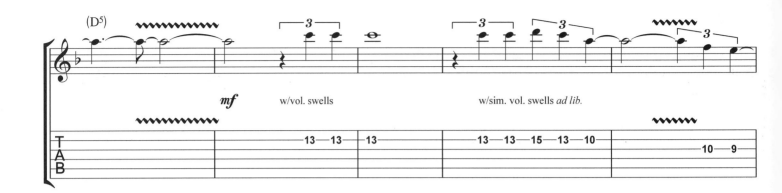

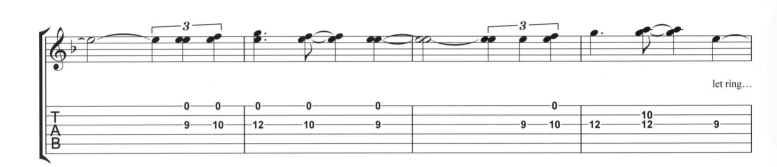

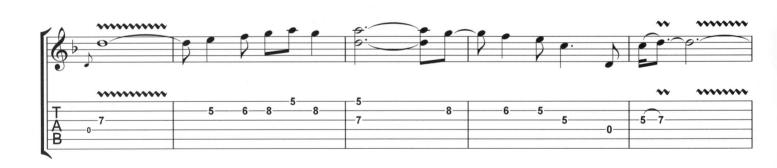

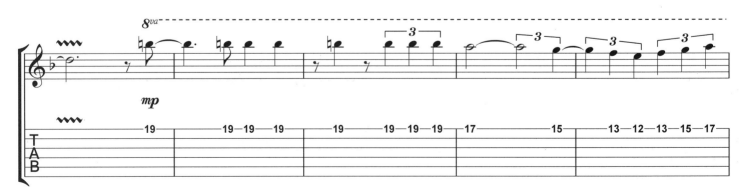

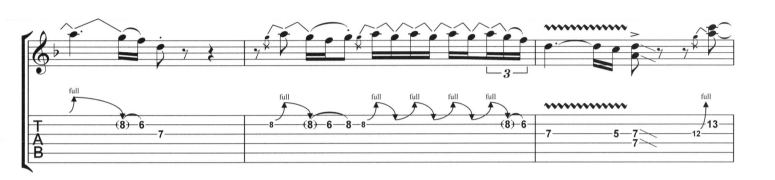

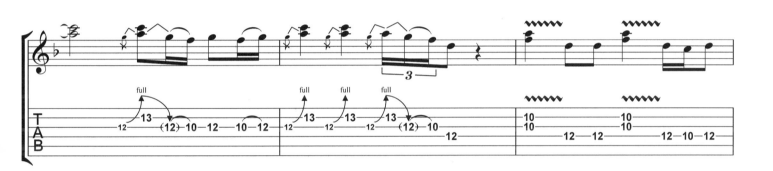

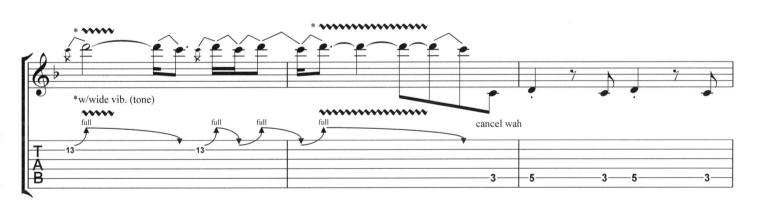

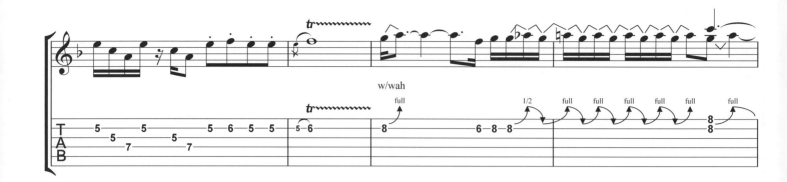

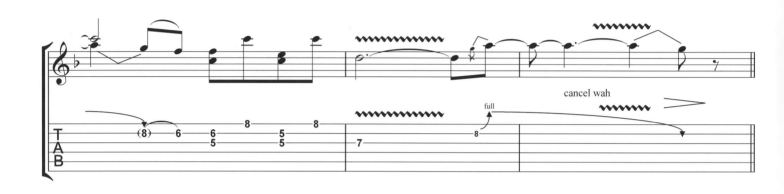

Bridge

05:24 (Gm)   (C)

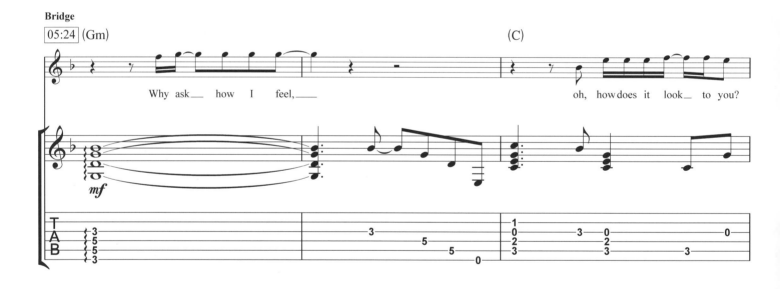

Why ask___ how I feel,___   oh, how does it look___ to you?

(G/B)   (Am)

I fell hook, line and sink - er,   lost my

116

cap-tain and my crew.   I'm stand-ing on the land-

-ing,   there's no-one there but me.

That's where you'll find me,   look-ing out on the

deep blue sea.

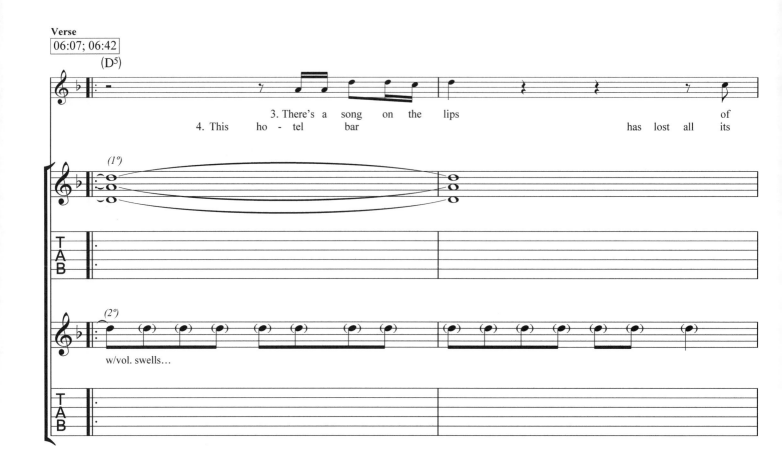

3. There's a song on the lips of
4. This ho - tel bar has lost all its

ev - 'ry - bo - dy._____
peo - ple.

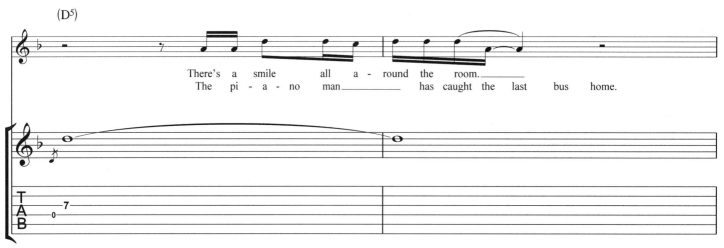

There's a smile all a - round the room._____
The pi - a - no man_____ has caught the last bus home.

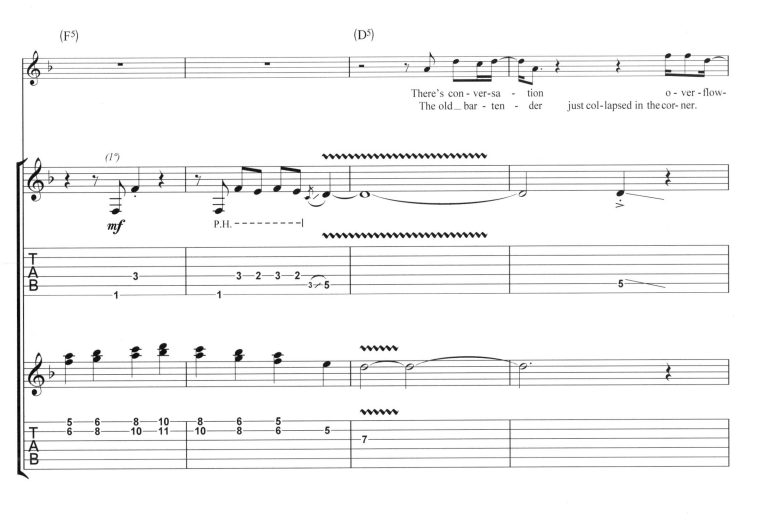

There's con - ver-sa - tion o - ver -flow-
The old— bar - ten - der just col-lapsed in the cor - ner.

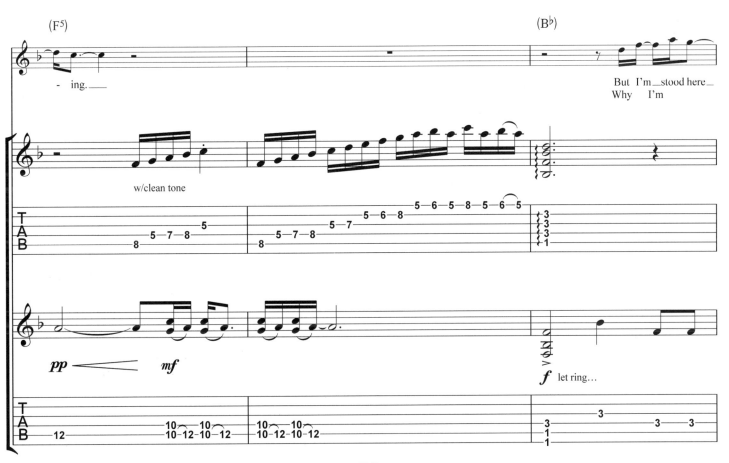

- ing. ____ But I'm—stood here—
Why I'm

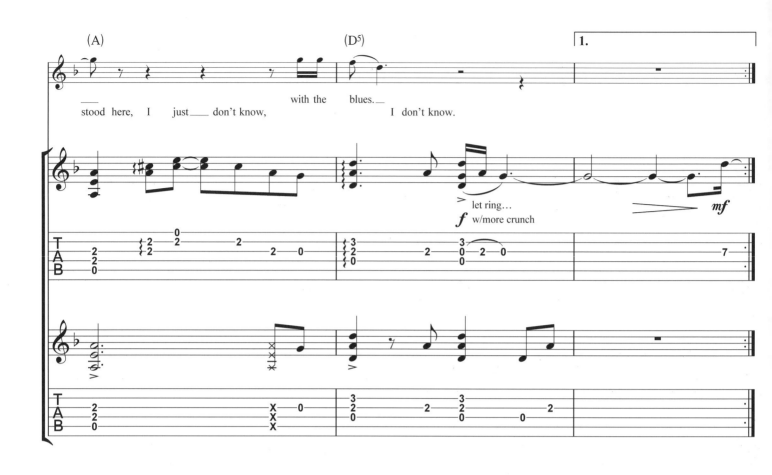

with the blues.

stood here, I just don't know, I don't know.

let ring...

f w/more crunch

2. **Chorus**

(F5)

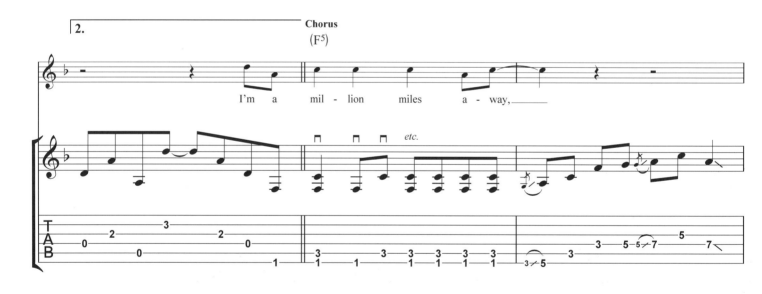

I'm a mil - lion miles a - way,

etc.

(D5) (B♭5)

I'm a mil-lion miles a - way. I'm sail - ing like the drift - wood

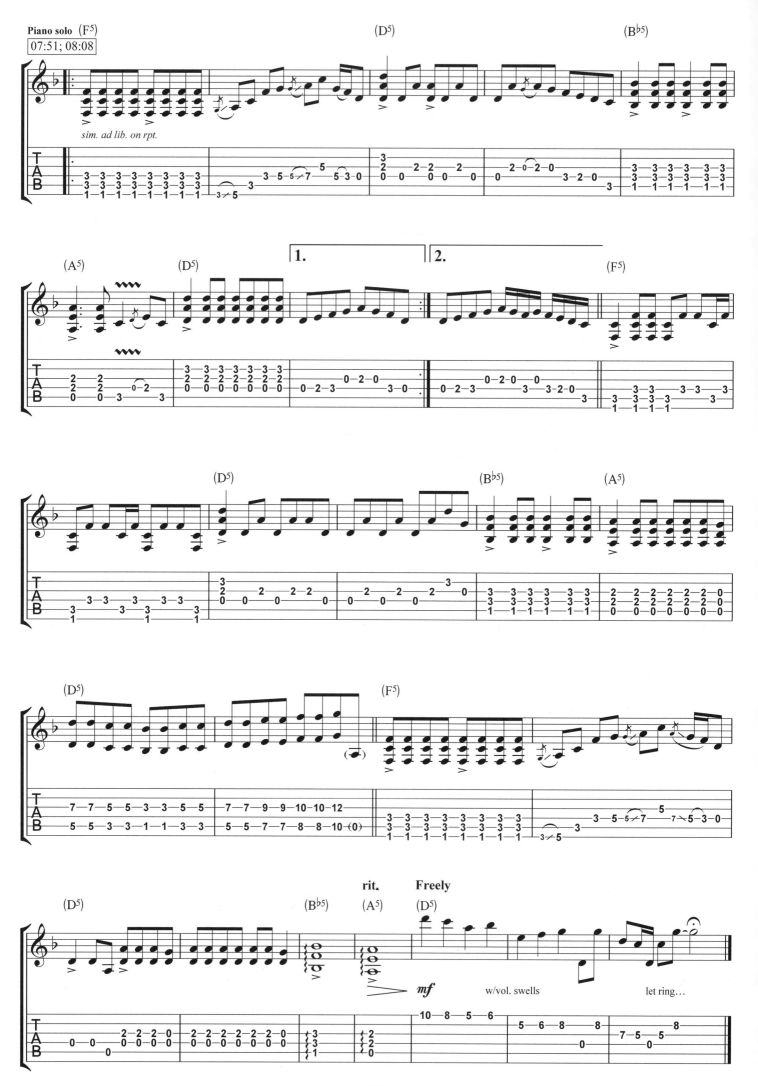

HANDS OFF

Words & Music by Rory Gallagher

Hands off,_____ now

here's a si - tu - a - tion, hands (off),_____ My girl needs con - sid - er - a - tion, hands off,__

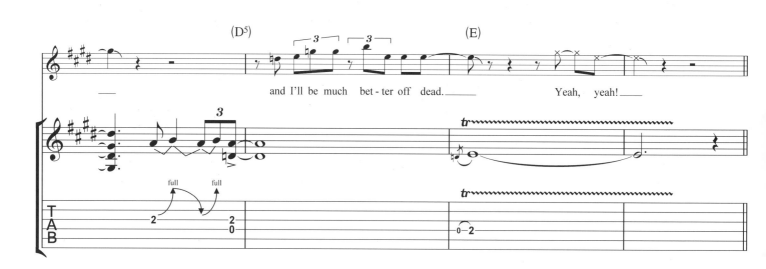

___ and I'll be much bet - ter off dead._____ Yeah, yeah!___

Solo

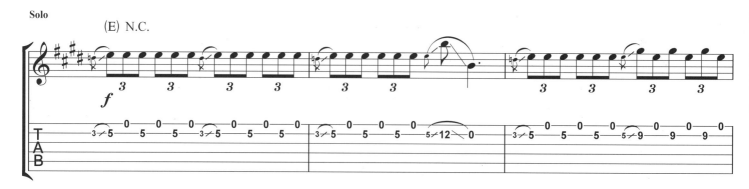

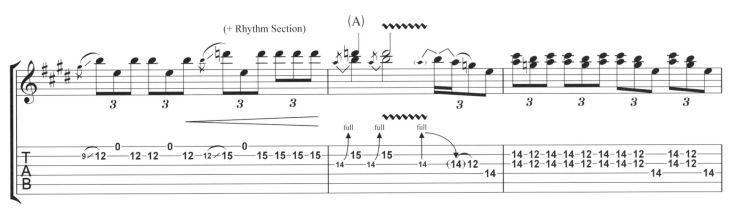

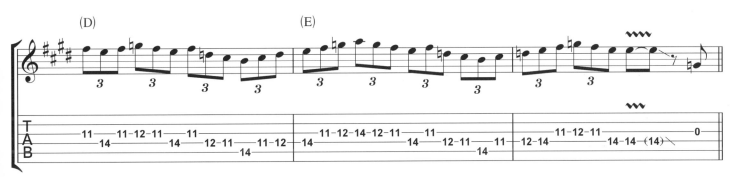

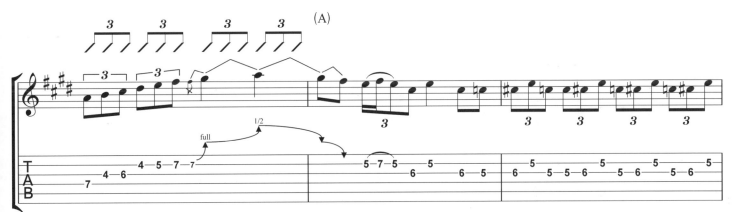

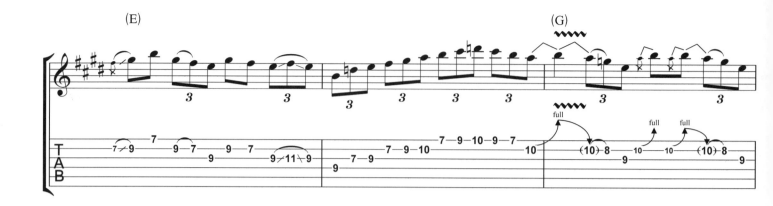

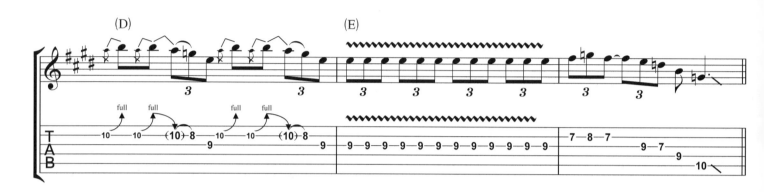

Piano break

01:45; 02:05

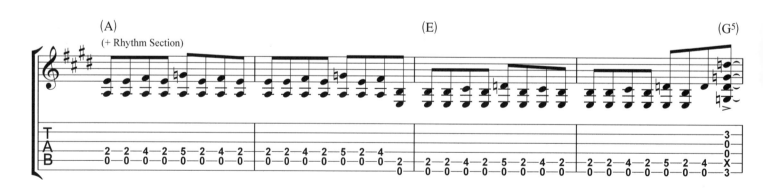

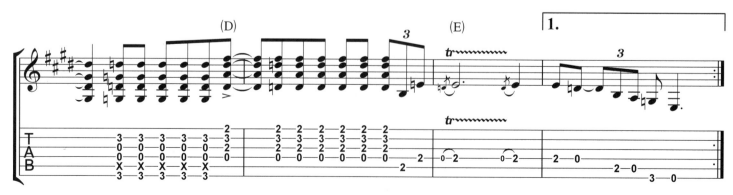

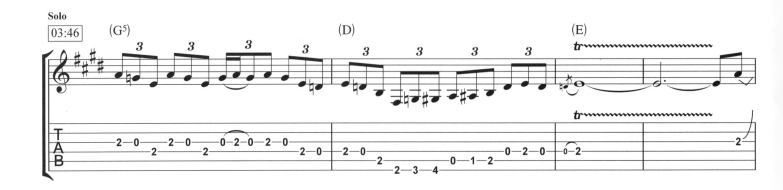

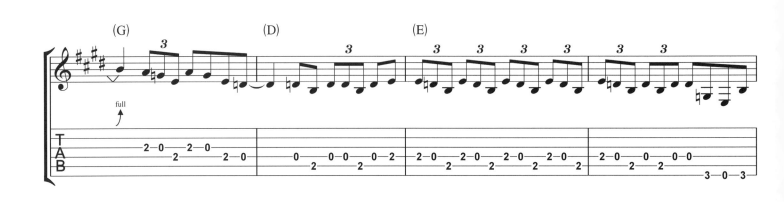

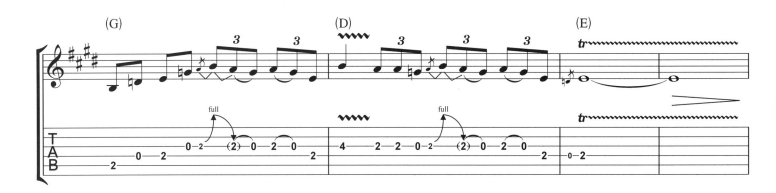

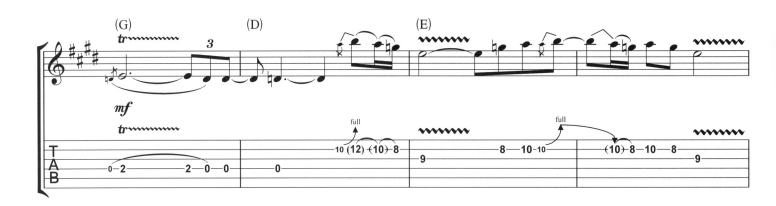

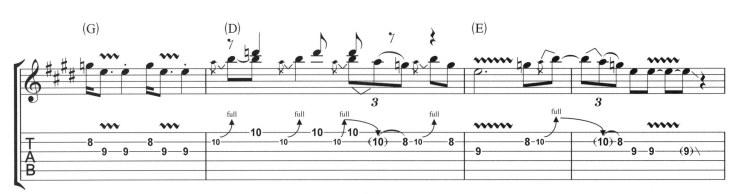

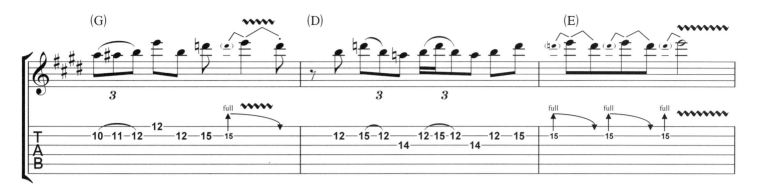

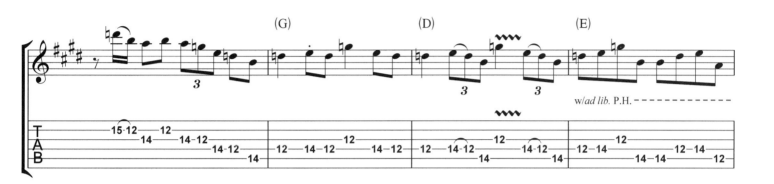

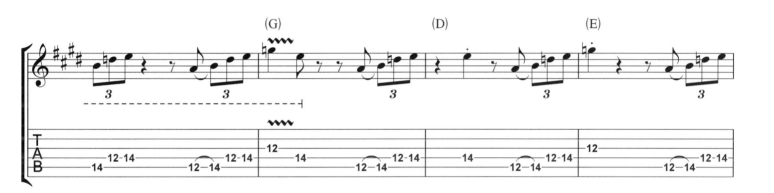

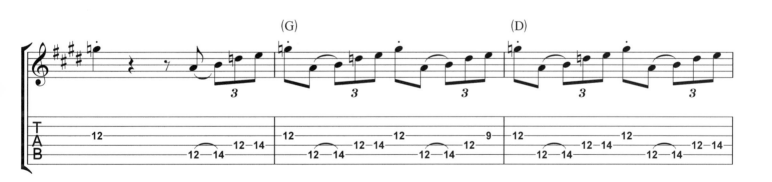

131

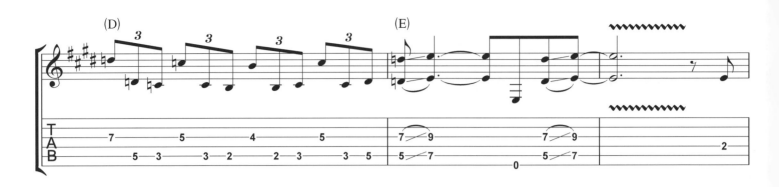

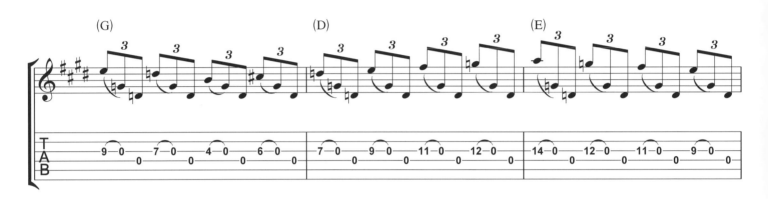

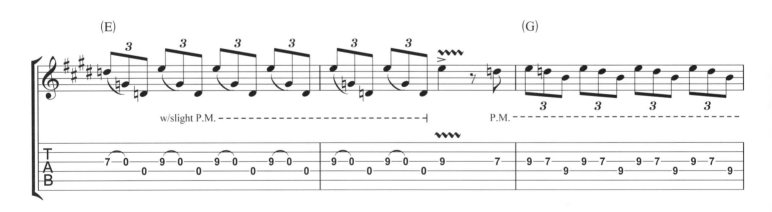

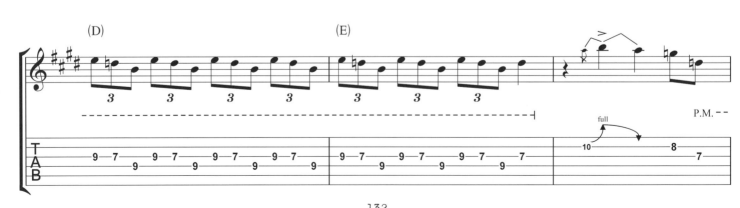

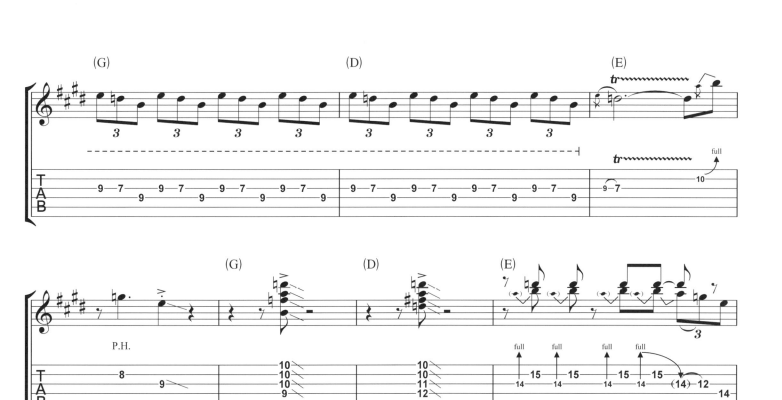

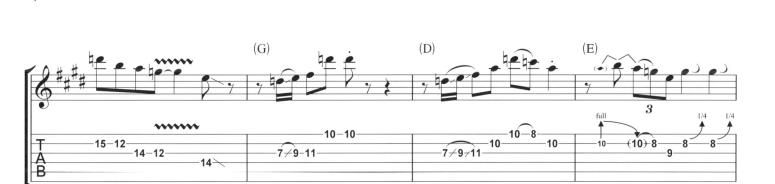

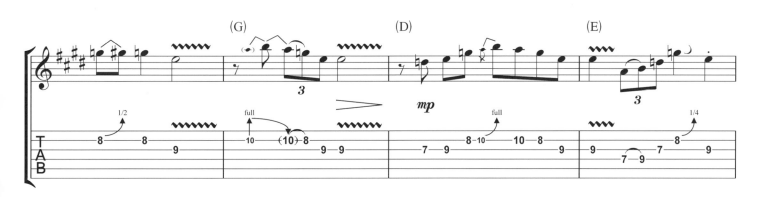

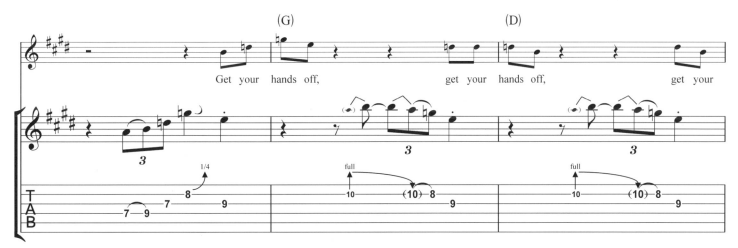

Get your hands off,   get your hands off,   get your

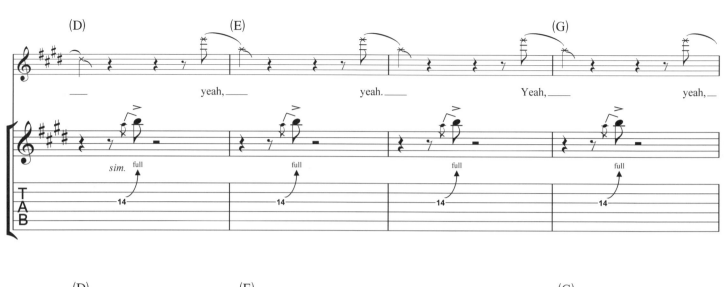

yeah,___ yeah.___ Yeah,___ yeah,___

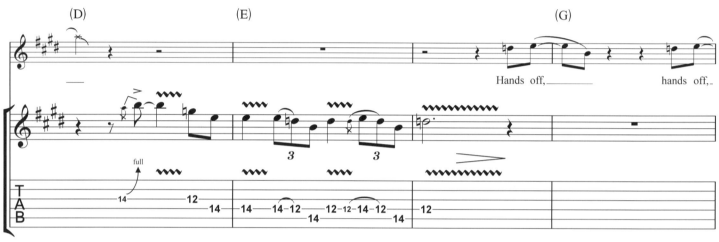

Hands off,_____ hands off,_

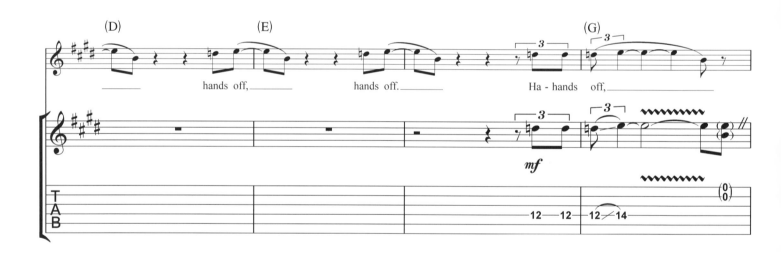

___ hands off,_____ hands off._____ Ha - hands off,_____

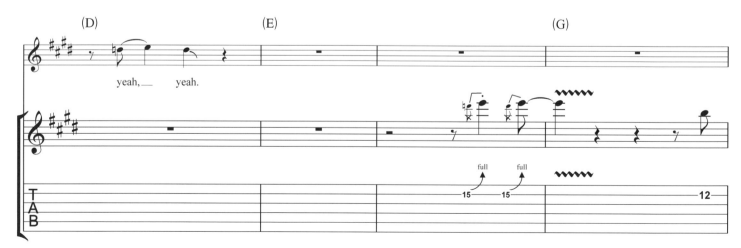

yeah,___ yeah.

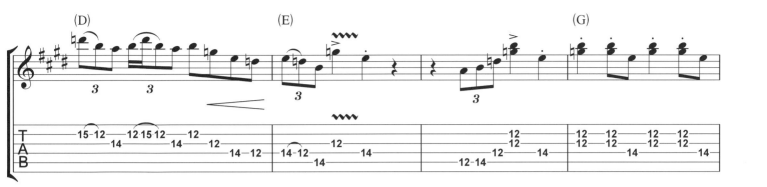

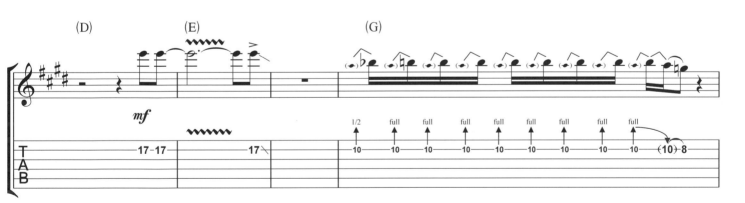

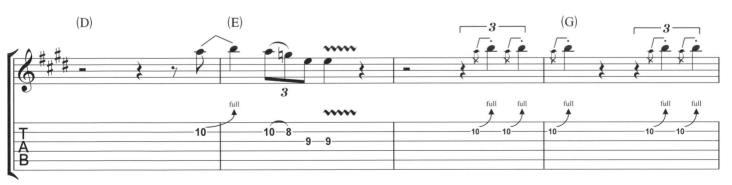

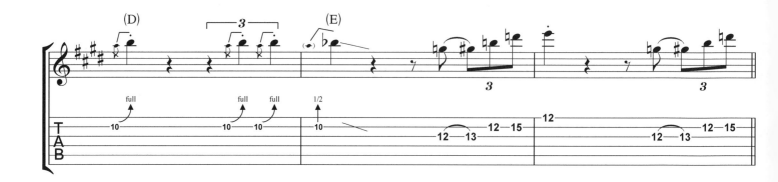

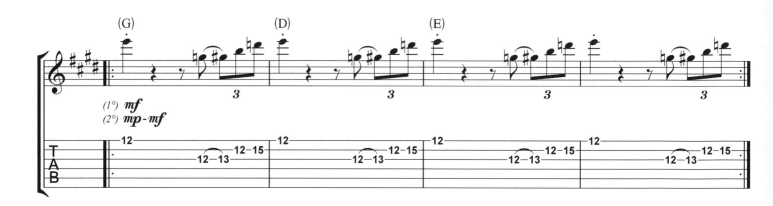

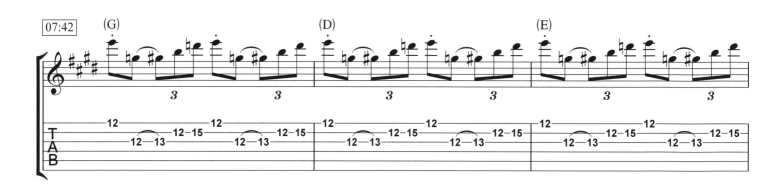

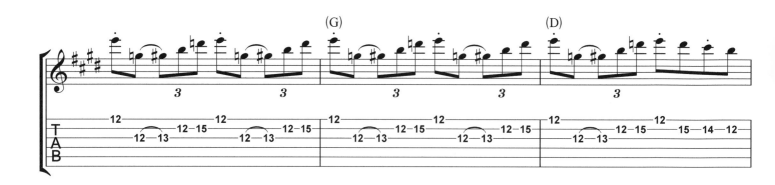

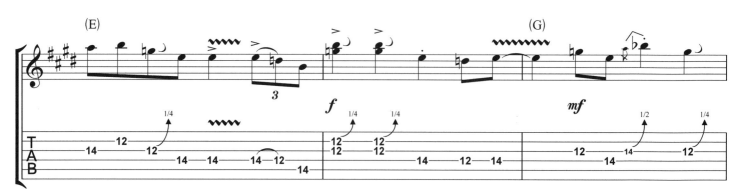

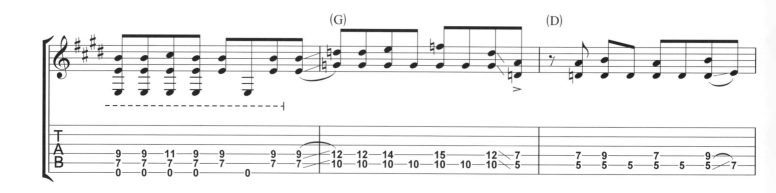

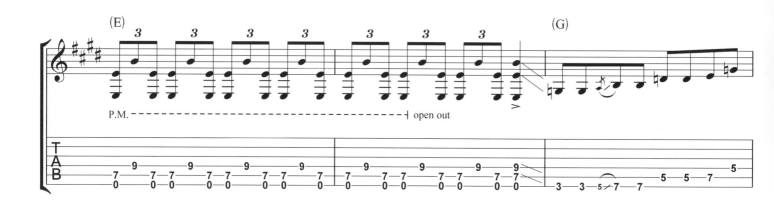

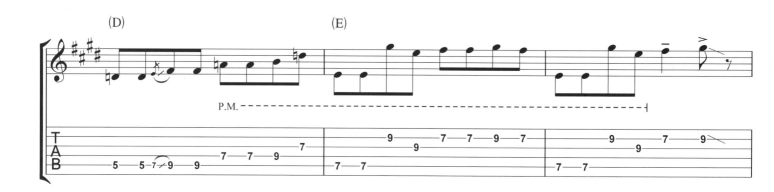

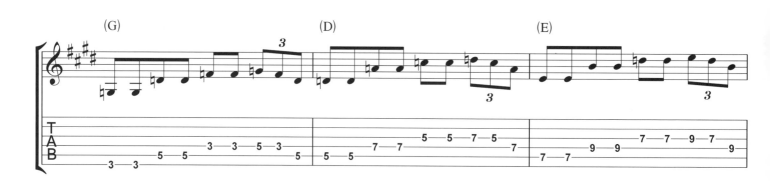

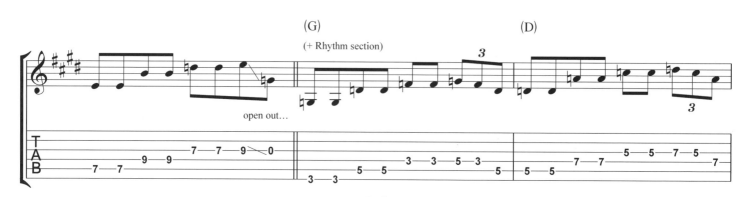

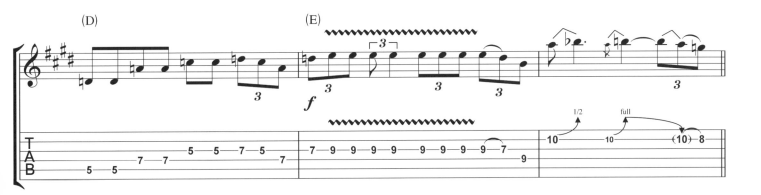

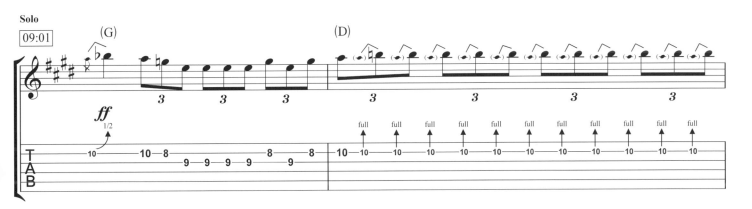

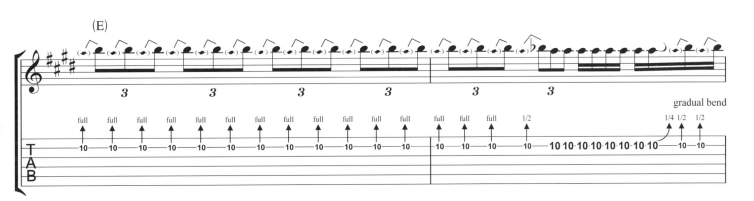

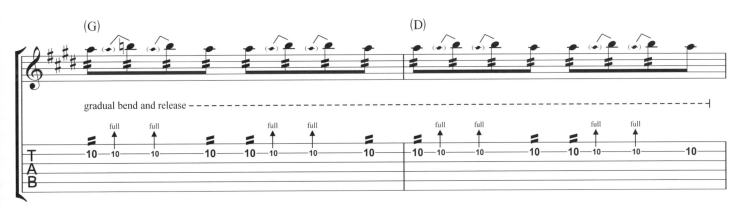

141

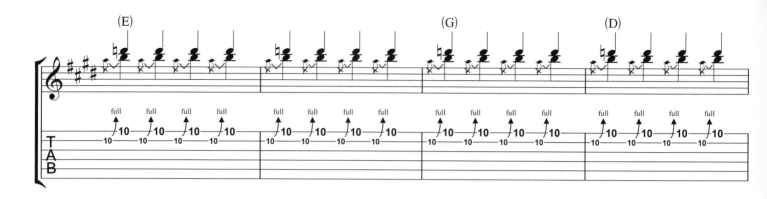

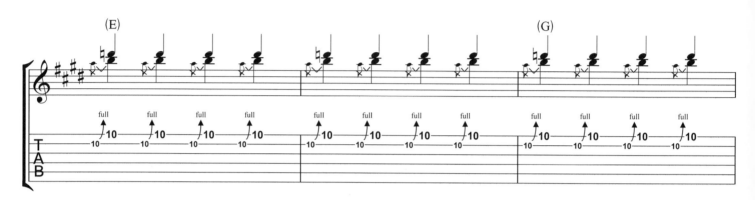

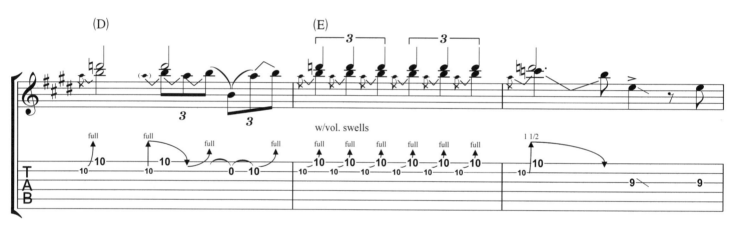

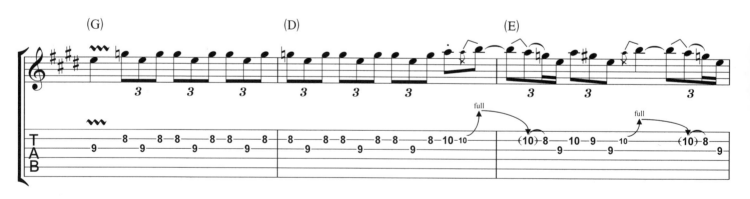

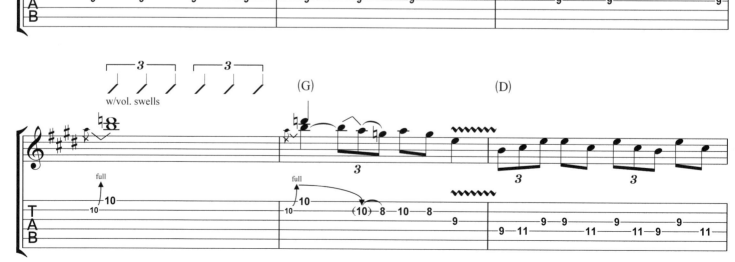

142

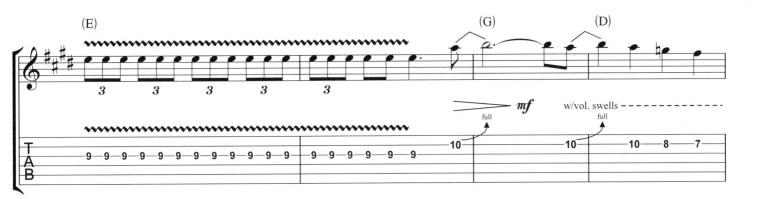

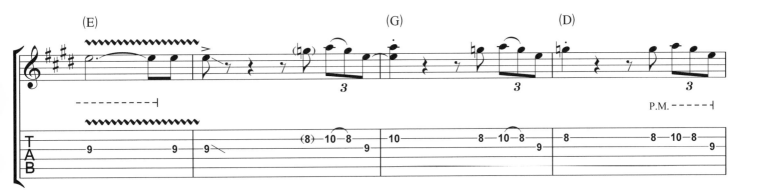

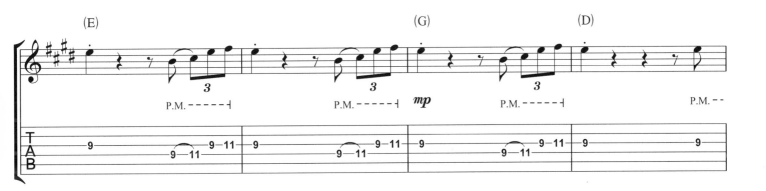

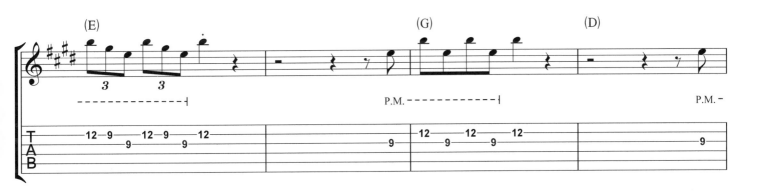

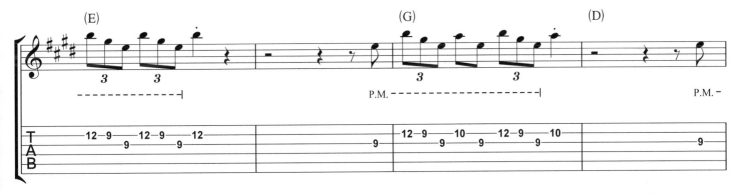

143

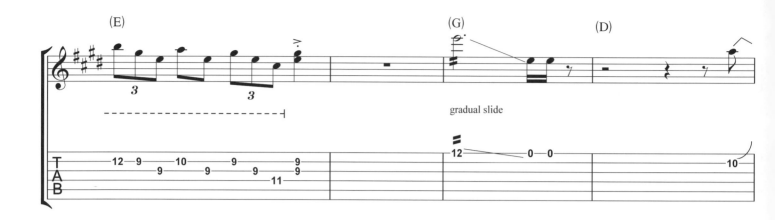

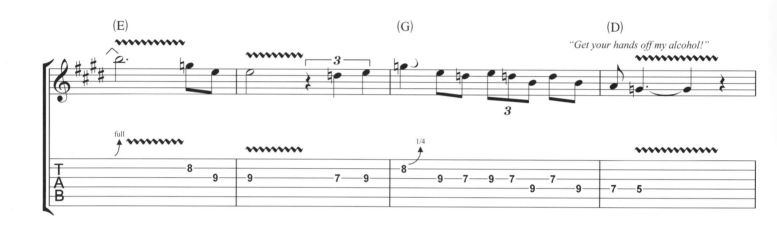

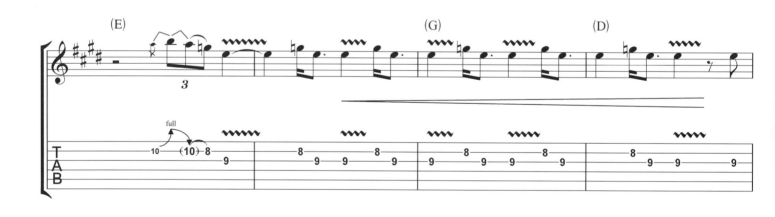

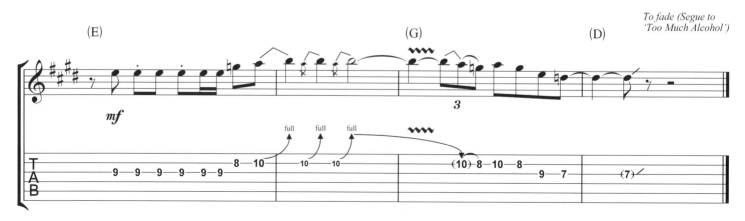

TOO MUCH ALCOHOL

Words & Music by J.B. Hutto

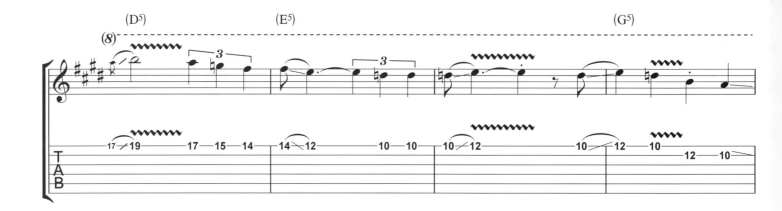

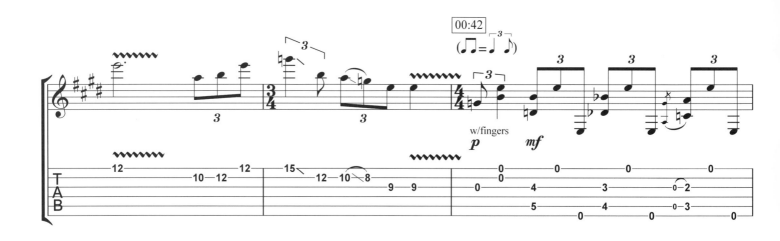

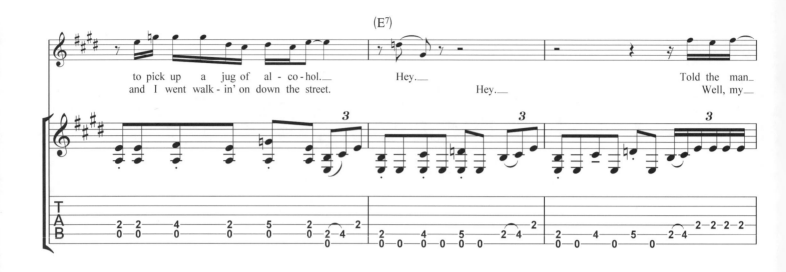

to pick up a jug of al-co-hol.__
and I went walk-in' on down the street.

Hey.__

Hey.__

Told the man__
Well, my__

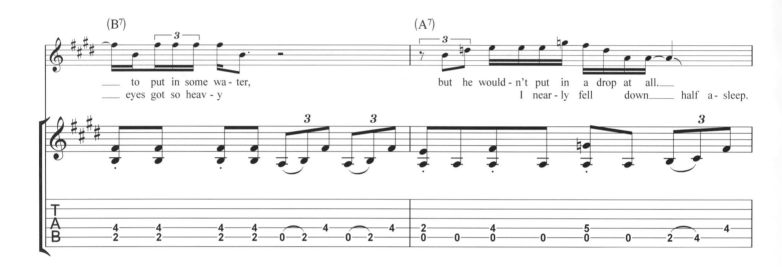

__ to put in some wa-ter,
__ eyes got so heav-y

but he would-n't put in a drop at all.__
I near-ly fell down__ half a-sleep.

1.

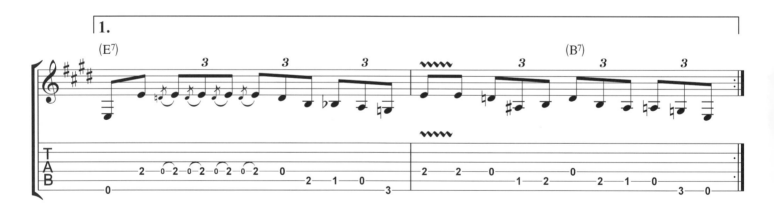

2.

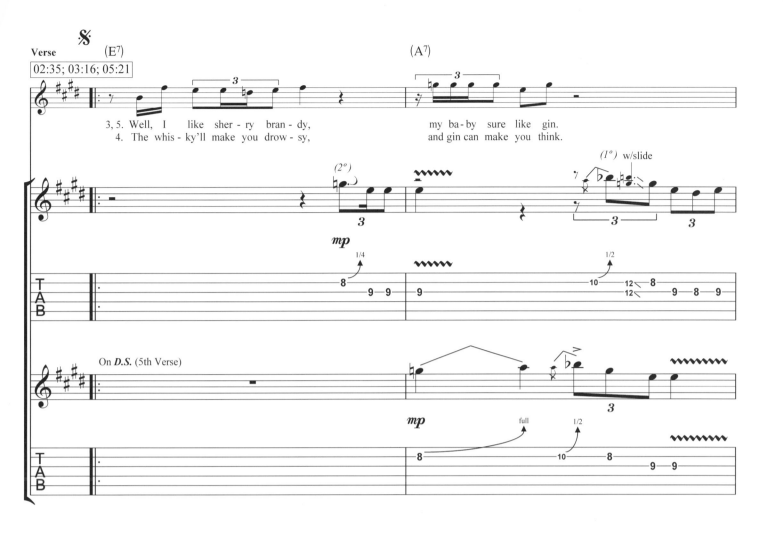

Verse (E⁷) (A⁷)

02:35; 03:16; 05:21

3, 5. Well, I like sher - ry bran - dy, my ba - by sure like gin.
4. The whis - ky'll make you drow - sy, and gin can make you think.

On *D.S.* (5th Verse)

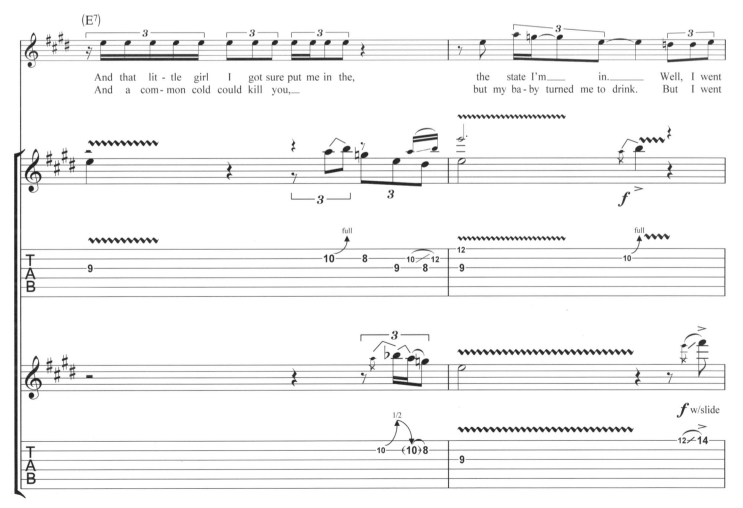

(E⁷) (A⁷)

And that lit - tle girl I got sure put me in the, the state I'm in. Well, I went
And a com - mon cold could kill you, but my ba - by turned me to drink. But I went

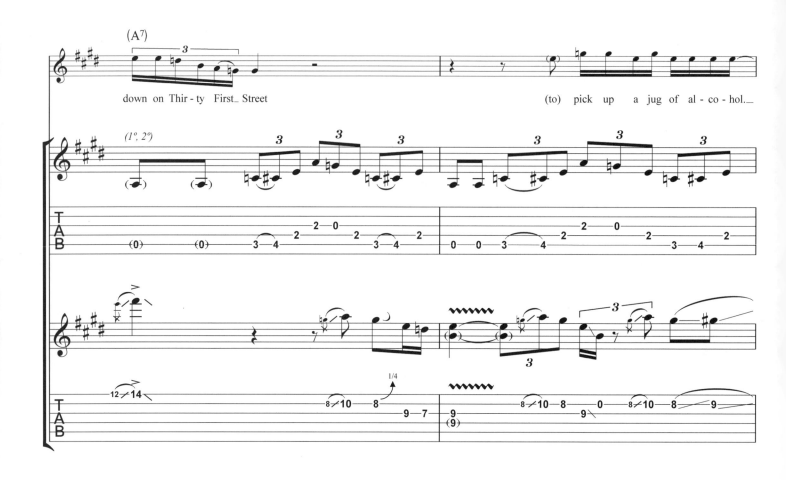

down on Thir - ty First_ Street   (to) pick up   a jug of al - co - hol._

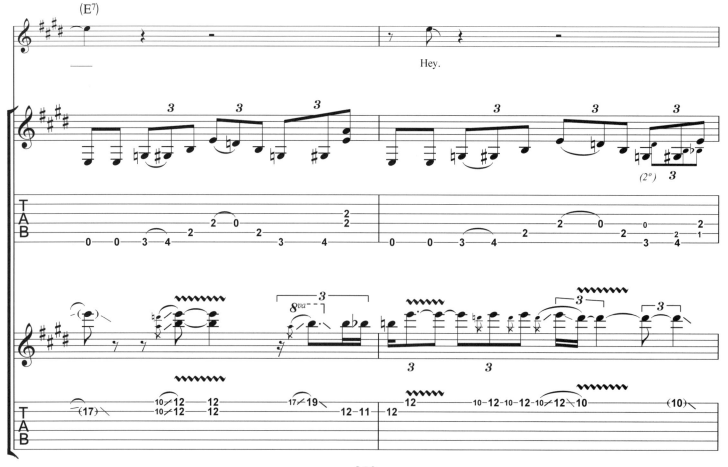

Hey.

150

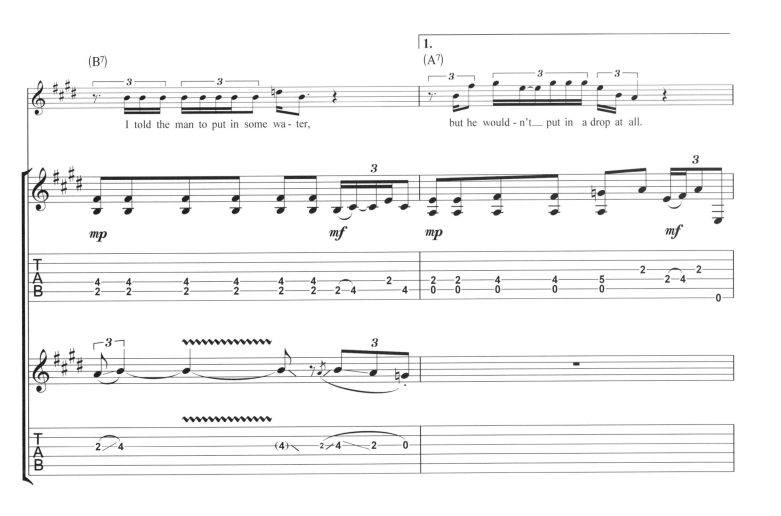

1.

I told the man to put in some wa - ter,   but he would - n't___ put in a drop at all.

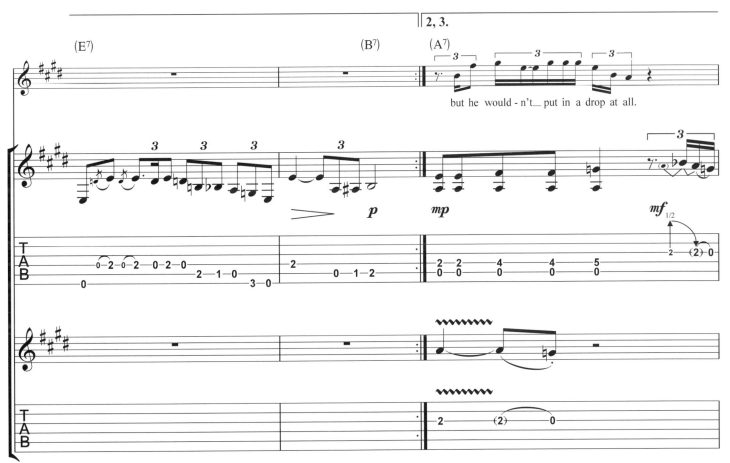

2, 3.

but he would - n't___ put in a drop at all.

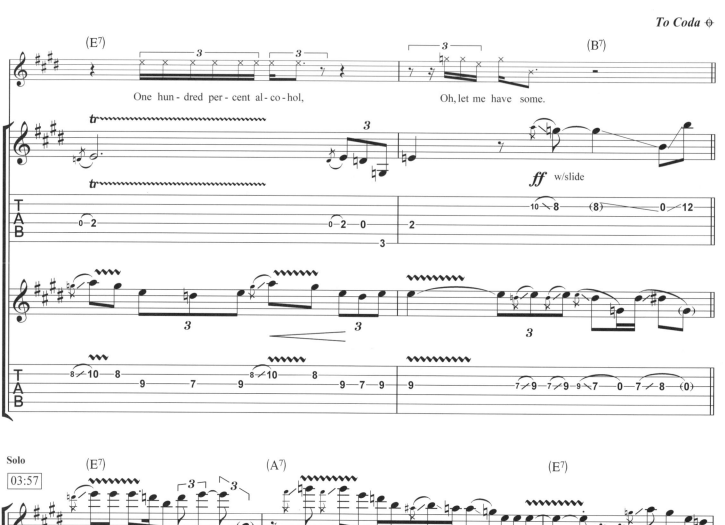

One hun - dred per - cent al - co - hol,   Oh, let me have some.

Solo

03:57

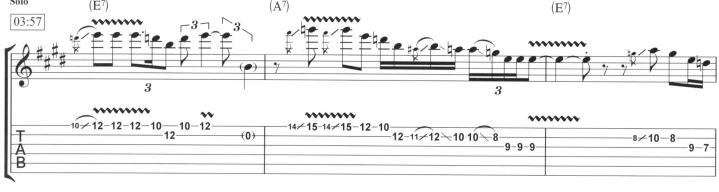

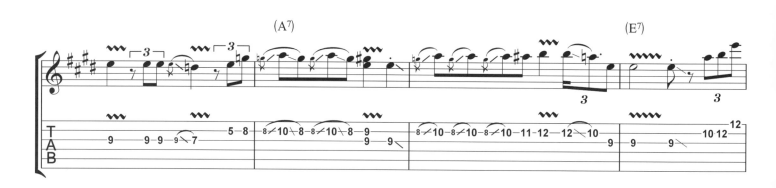

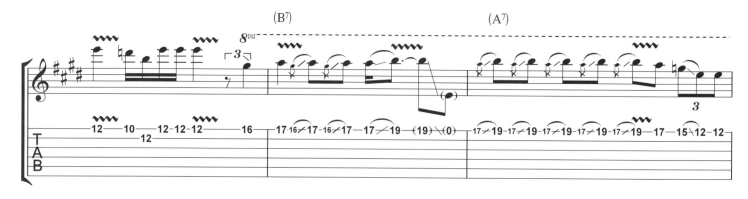

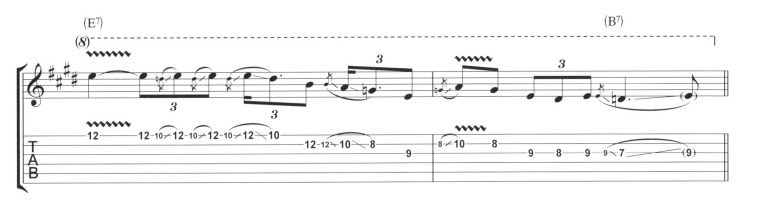

Piano Solo

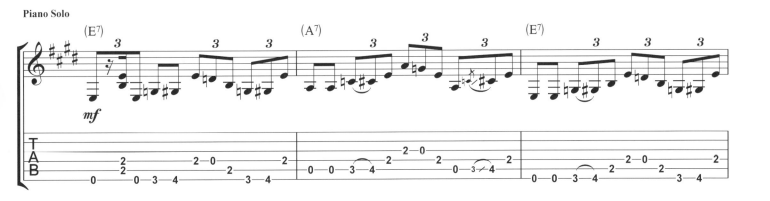

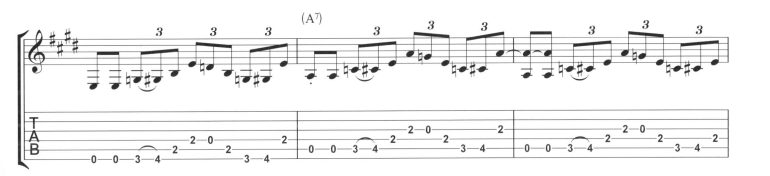

D.S. al Coda

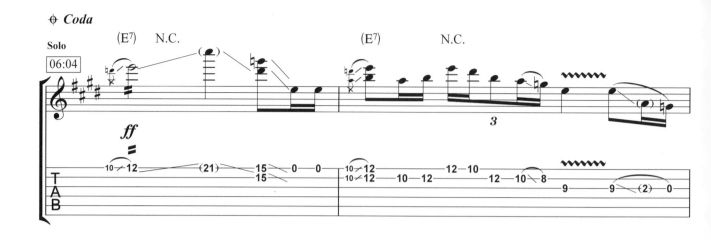

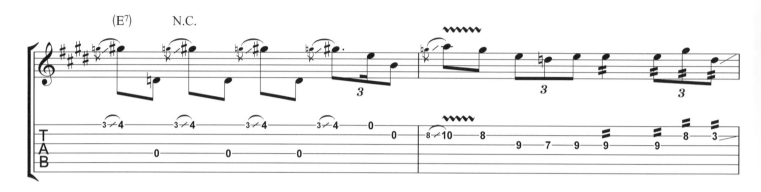

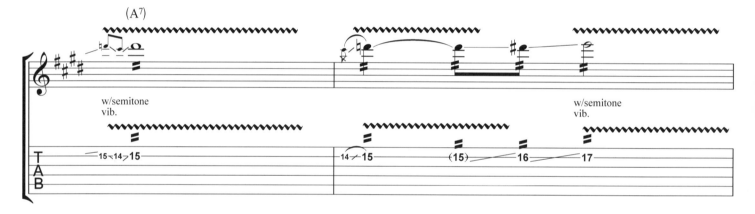

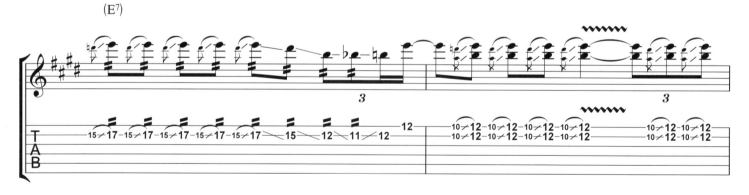

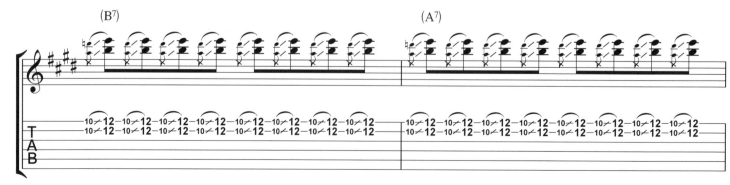

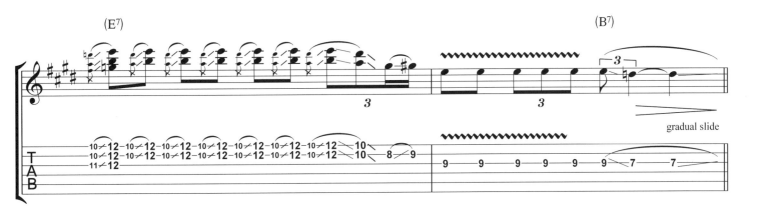

Verse

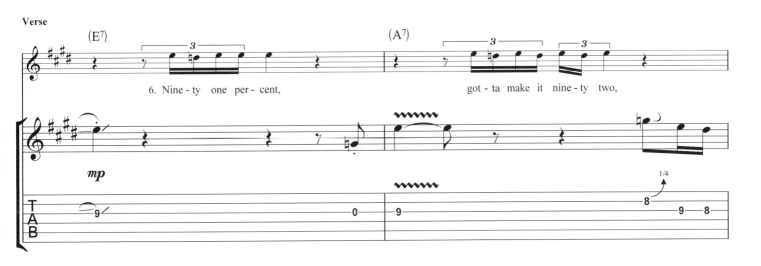

6. Nine-ty one per-cent, got-ta make it nine-ty two,

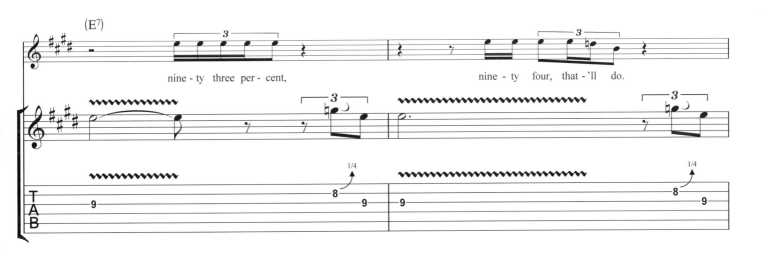

nine-ty three per-cent, nine-ty four, that-'ll do.

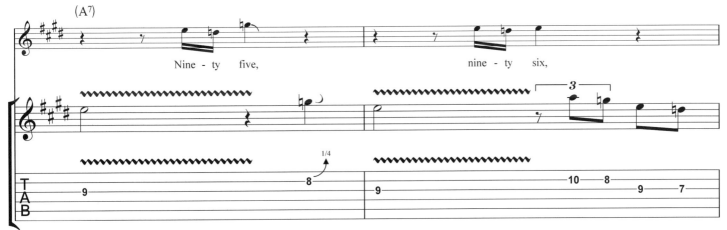

Nine-ty five, nine-ty six,

155

Freely

nine - ty se - ven per - cent,   nine - ty eight,

bar - ten - der, that's nine - ty nine.   Make it one hun - dred per - cent,

one hun - dred per - cent,   one hun - dred per - cent.

Wan - na try some?   Wan - na try some?

One hun - dred per - cent.   And I won't feel a thing_ at all._

rall.

w/fingers

07:56   **Freely**

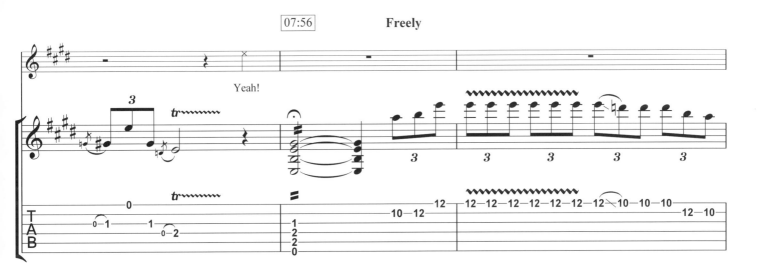

Yeah!

(E⁵)

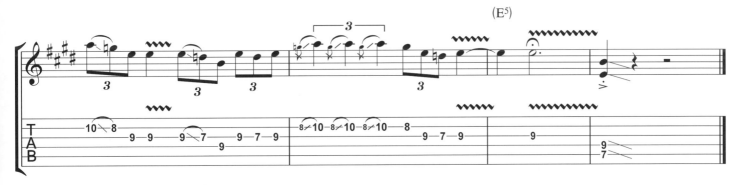

WHO'S THAT COMING

Words & Music by Rory Gallagher

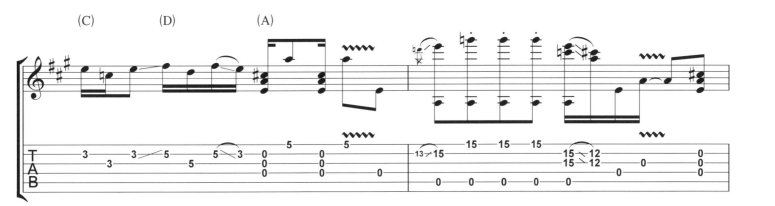

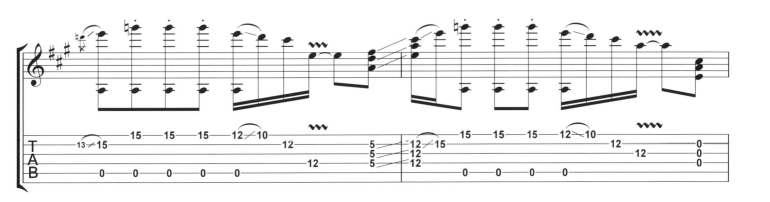

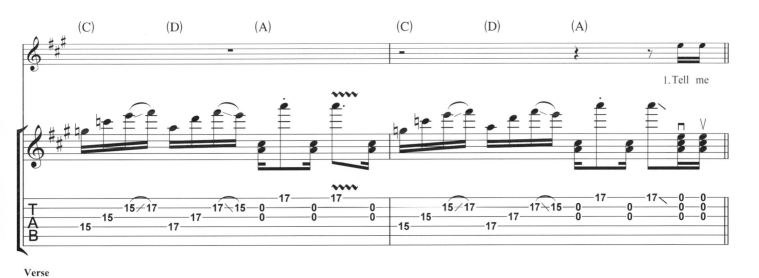

Verse

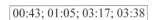

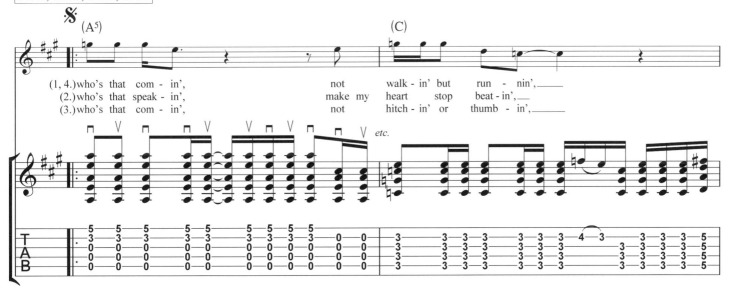

(1, 4.) who's that com - in',   not   walk - in' but   run - nin', _____
(2.) who's that speak - in',   make my   heart stop   beat - in', __
(3.) who's that com - in',   not   hitch - in' or   thumb - in', _____

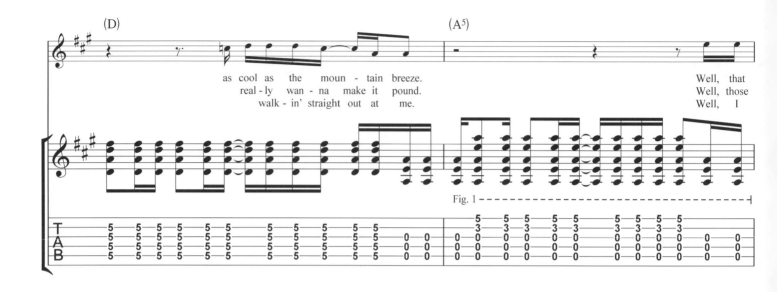

as cool as the moun - tain breeze.
real - ly wan - na make it pound.
walk - in' straight out at me.

Well, that
Well, those
Well, I

Fig. 1

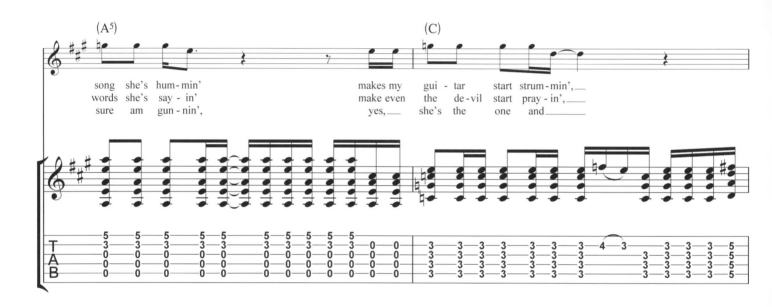

song she's hum - min'
words she's say - in'
sure am gun - nin',

makes my gui - tar start strum - min',
make even the de - vil start pray - in',
yes, she's the one and

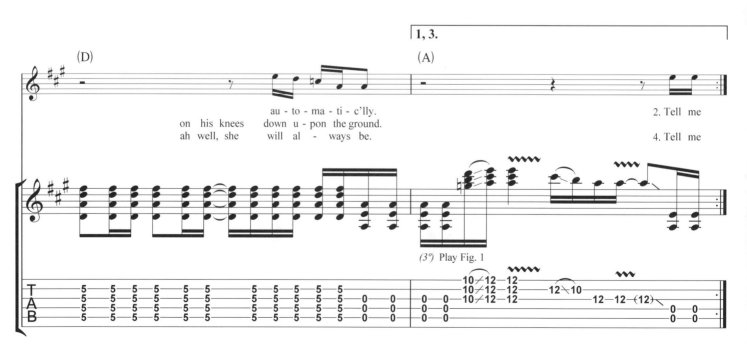

1, 3.

au - to - ma - ti - c'lly.
on his knees down u - pon the ground.
ah well, she will al - ways be.

2. Tell me
4. Tell me

(3°) Play Fig. 1

160

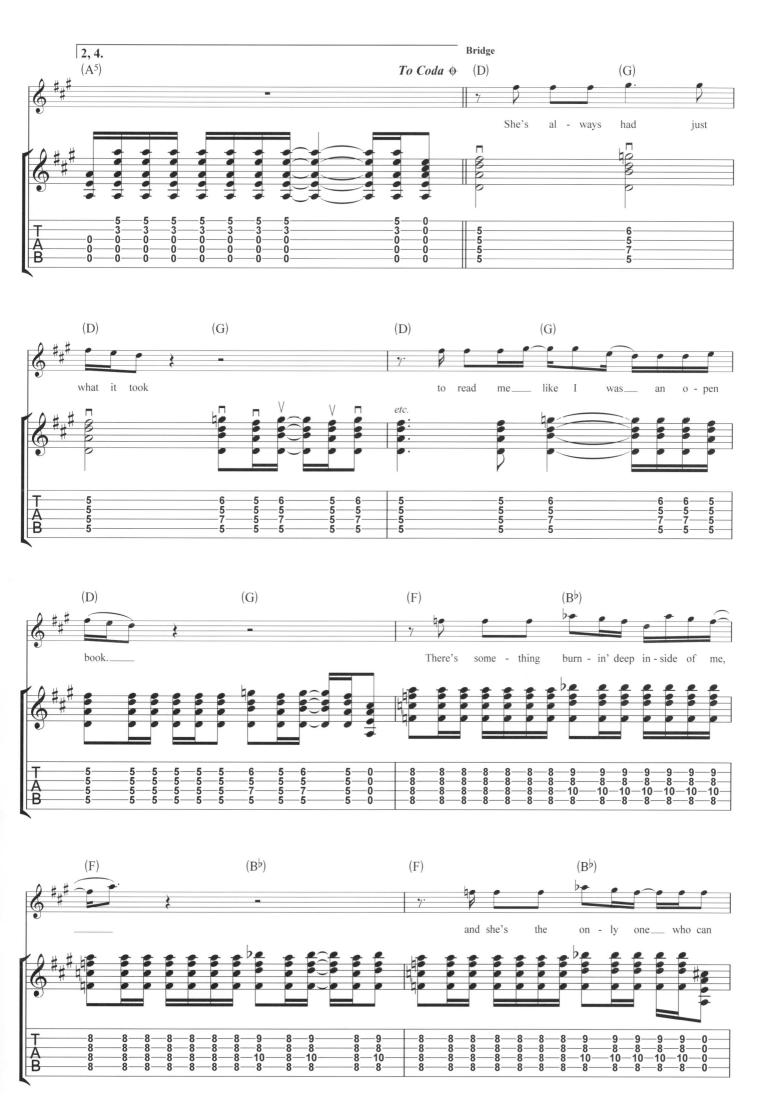

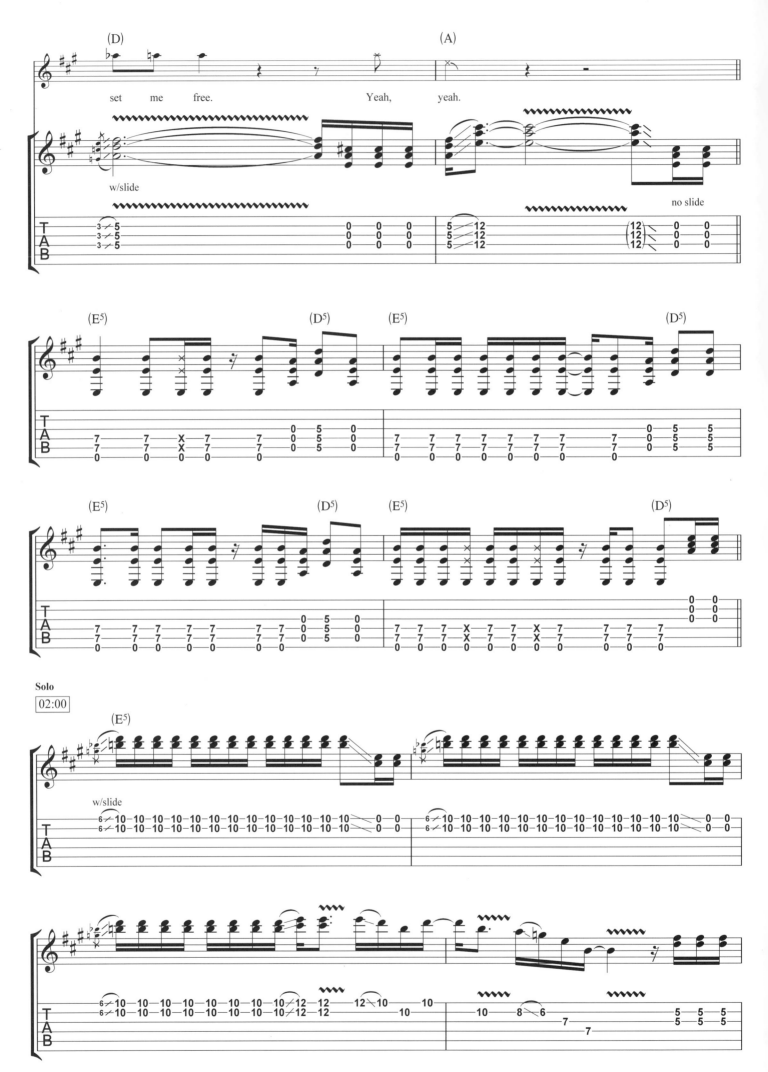

set me free. Yeah, yeah.

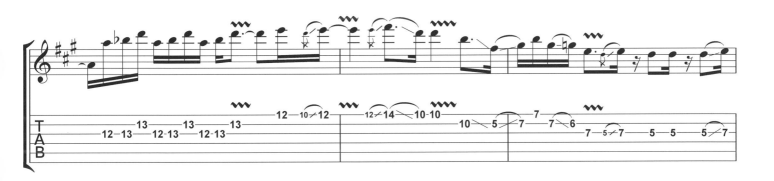

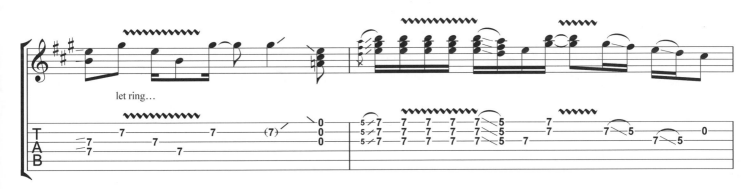

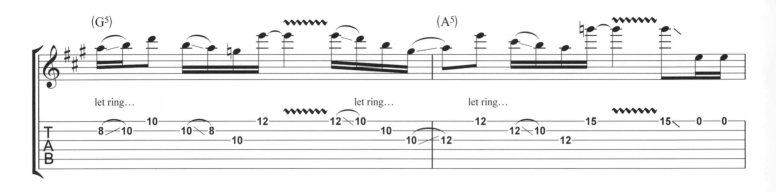

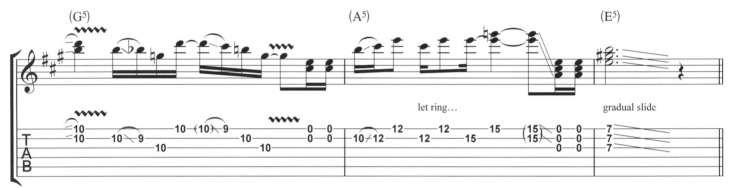

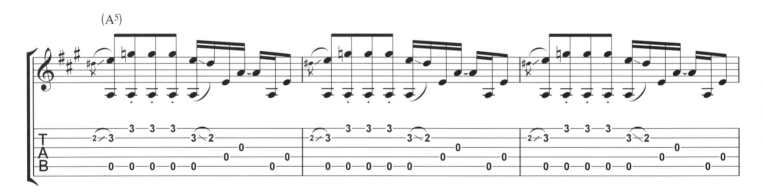

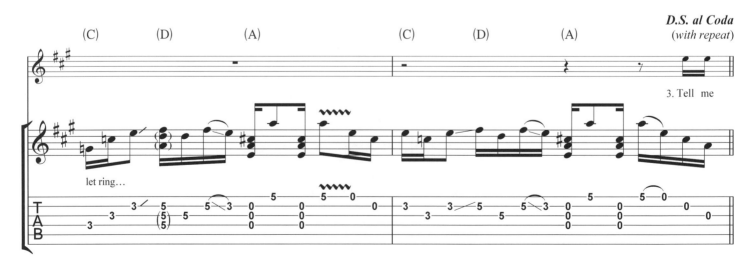

164

⊕ Coda

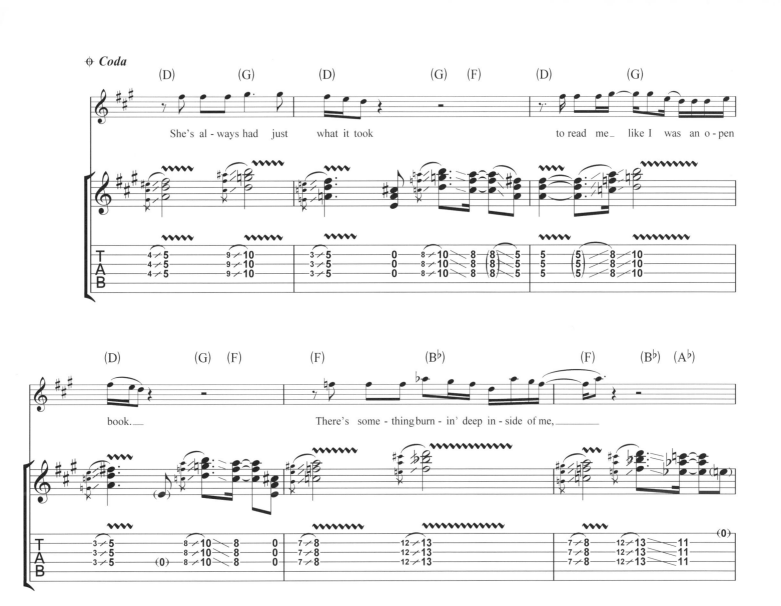

She's al-ways had just what it took to read me_ like I was an o-pen

book.___ There's some-thing burn-in' deep in-side of me,_____

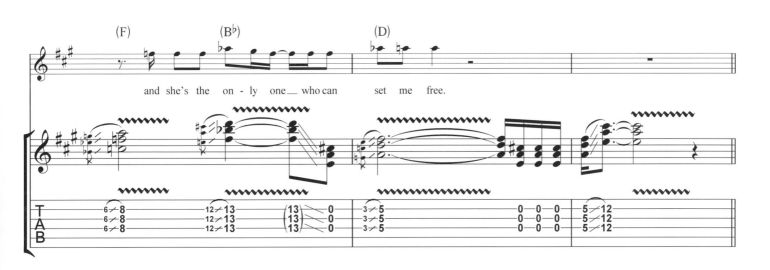

and she's the on-ly one_ who can set me free.

Piano solo

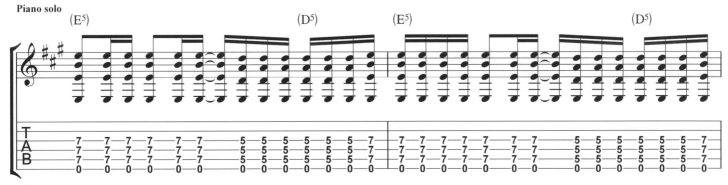

165

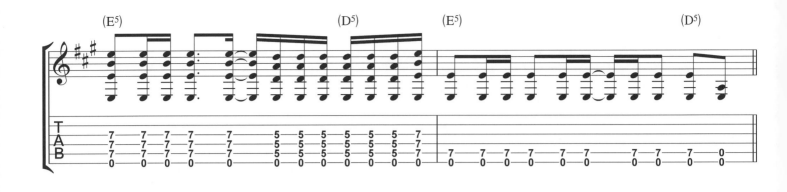

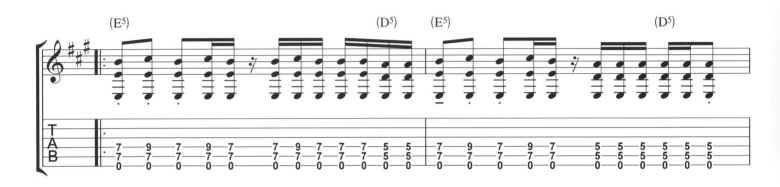

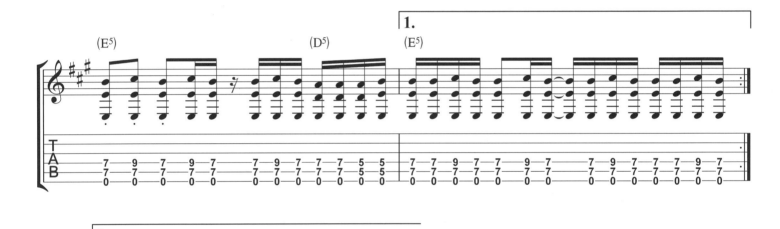

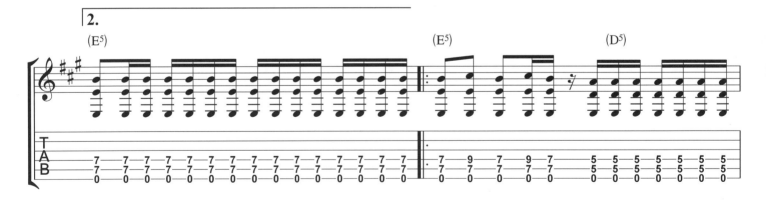

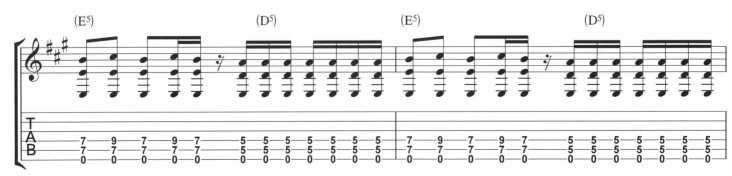

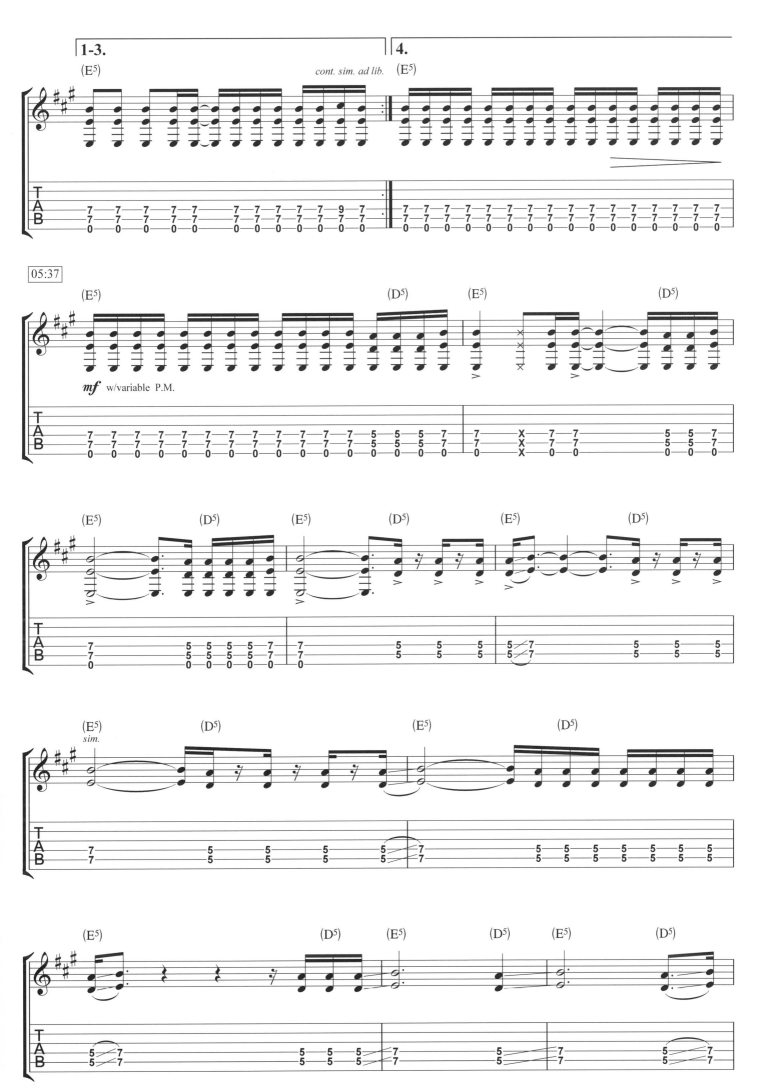

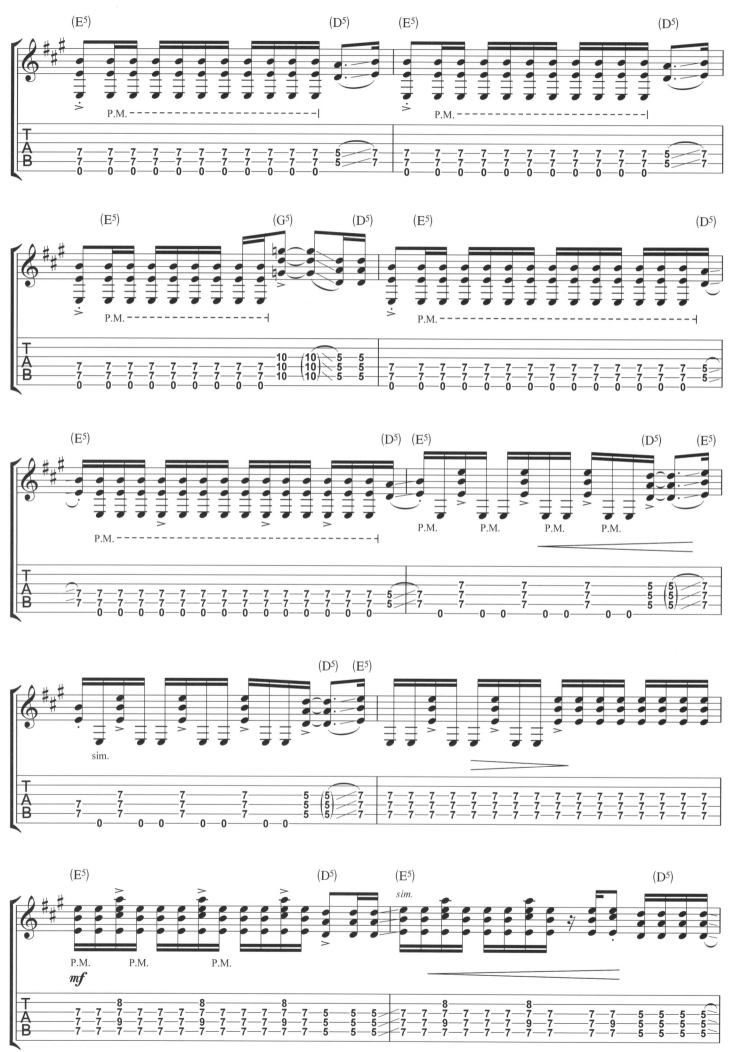

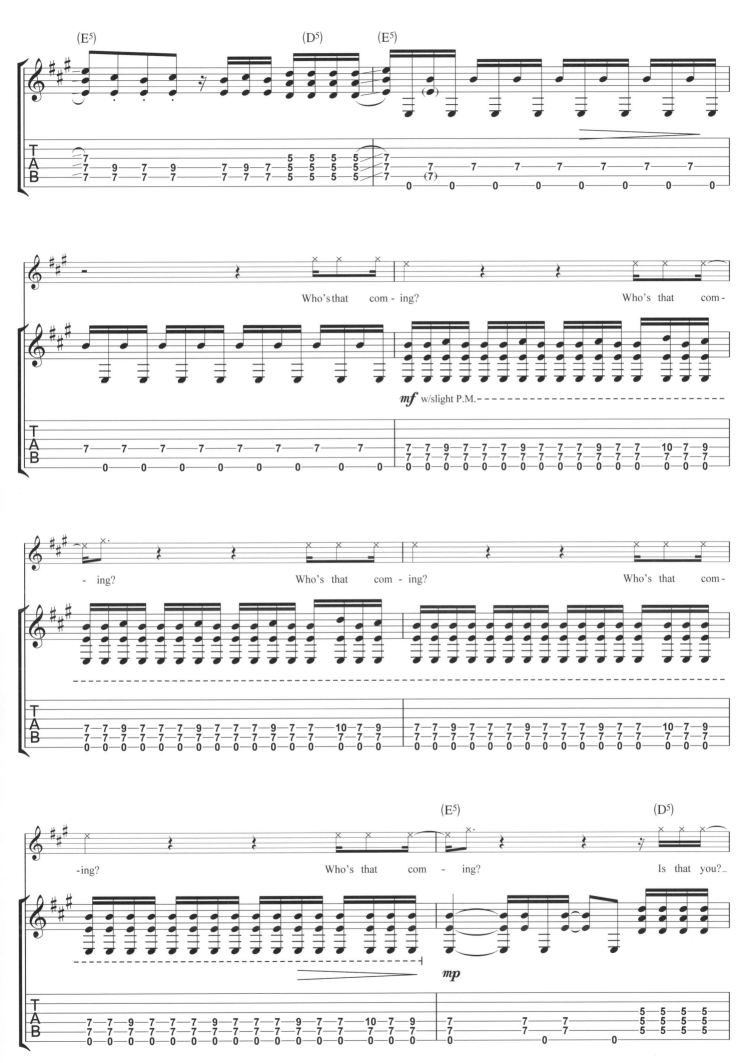

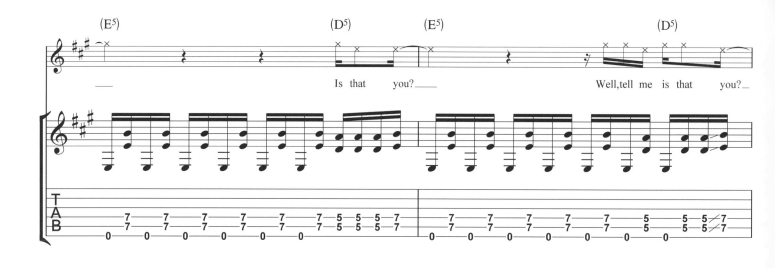

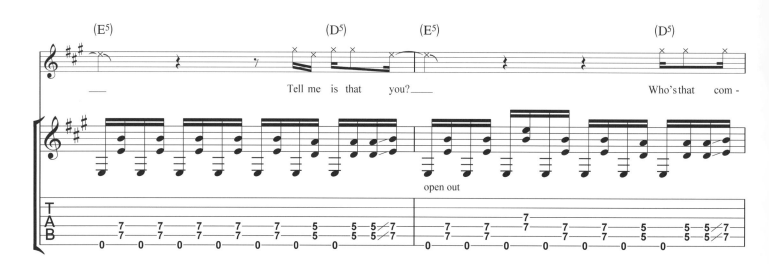

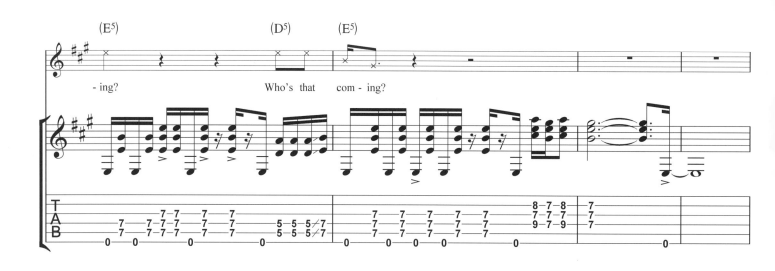

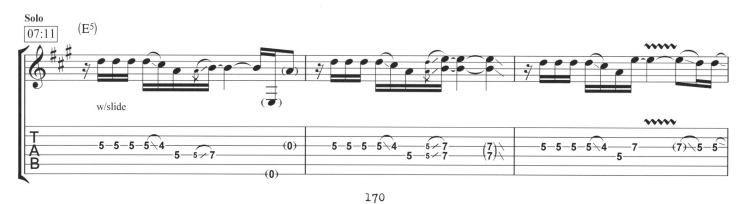

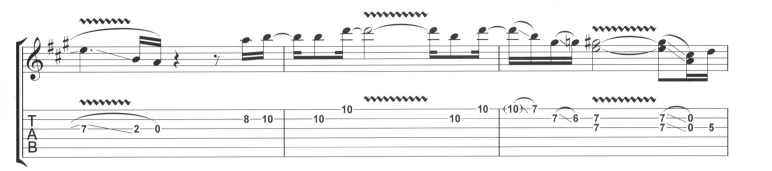

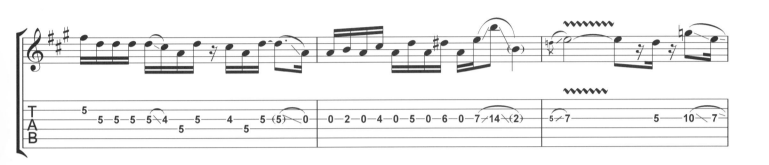

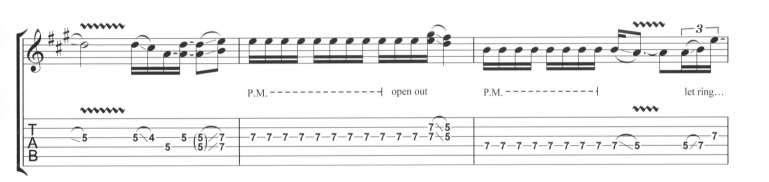

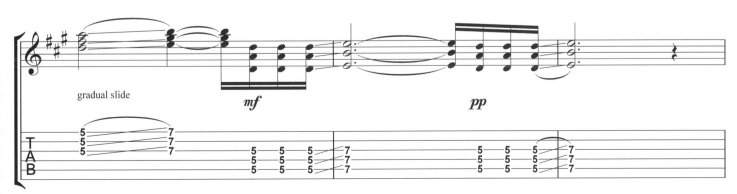

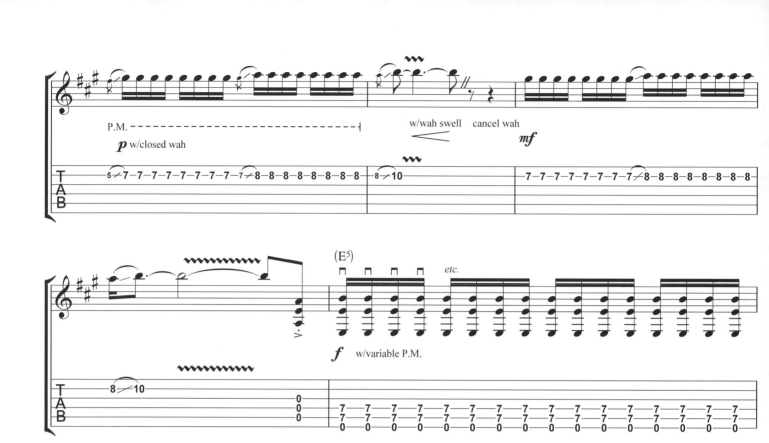

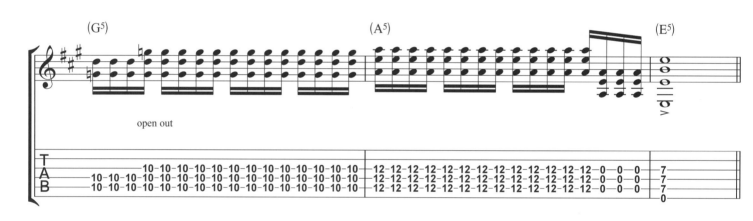

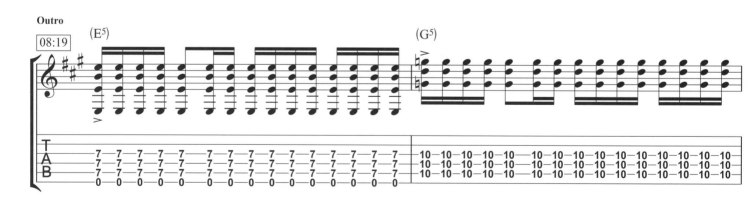

Outro

08:19

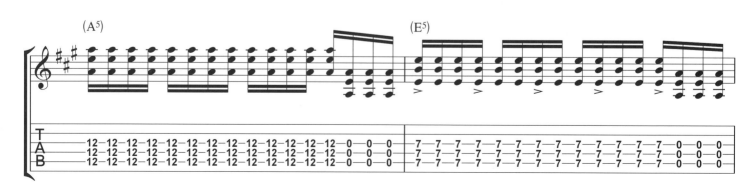

172

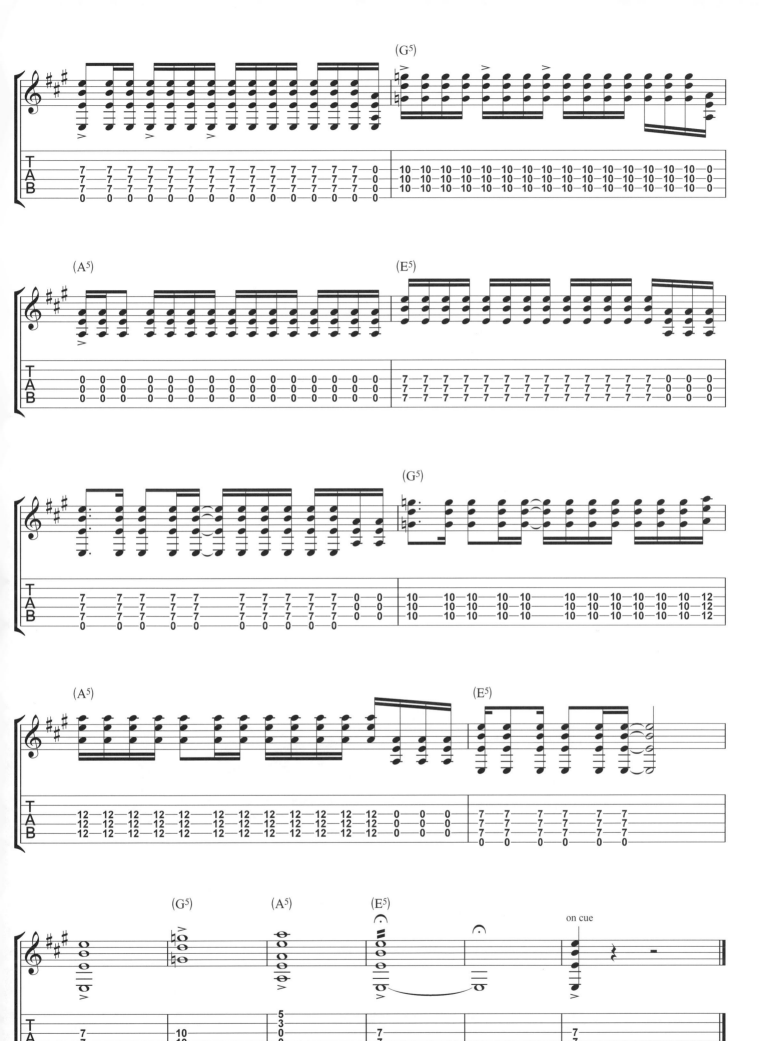

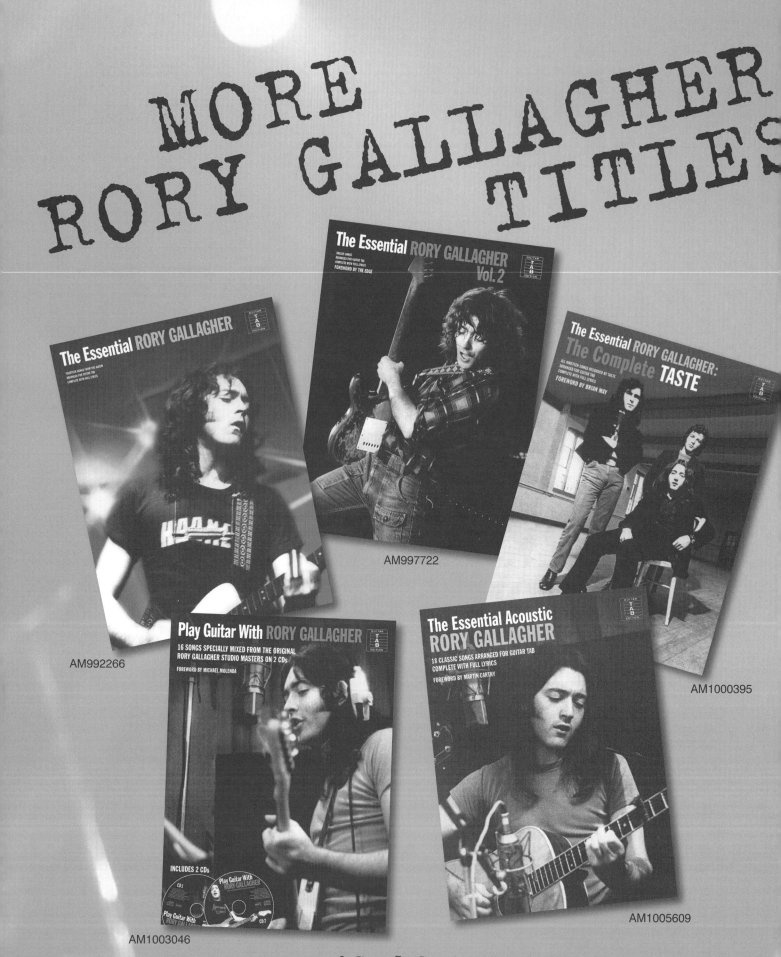

HOW TO DOWNLOAD
YOUR MUSIC TRACKS

1. Carefully remove your Download Card from the inside back cover of this book.

TO REDEEM THIS CARD VISIT
www.musicsalesdownloads.com

ENTER ACCESS CODE:

XXXXXXXXX

Download Cards are powered by Dropcards.
User must accept terms at dropcards.com/terms
which are adopted by The Music Sales Group.
Not redeemable for cash. Void where prohibited or restricted by law.

DCARD1006478

2. On the back of the card is your unique access code. Enter this at www.musicsalesdownloads.com

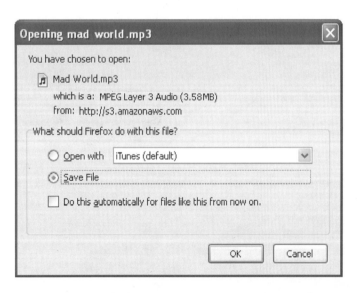

3. Follow the instructions to save your files to your computer*. That's it!

*Appearance of download manager will vary depending upon operating system and web browser.
In case of difficulty when downloading files, please contact dropcards.com/help
Card missing? Please contact music@musicsales.co.uk